Do Dead People Watch You Shower?

AND OTHER QUESTIONS YOU'VE BEEN
ALL BUT DYING TO ASK A MEDIUM

Concetta Bertoldi

MJF BOOKS
NEW YORK

Published by MJF Books
Fine Communications
322 Eighth Avenue
New York, NY 10001

Do Dead People Watch You Shower?
LC Control Number: 2016933221
ISBN 978-1-60671-347-1

Printed in the United States of America.

MJF Books and the MJF colophon are trademarks of Fine Creative Media, Inc.

QF   10 9 8 7 6 5 4 3 2 1

This book is dedicated to my very best dispatchers:
My father, Manny Ferrell, and my brother, Harold Ferrell

INTRODUCTION

I know you've got a lot of questions—after all, that's the reason you picked up this book, right? But before I get to those, I thought it might be good for you to know who it is who you're talking with, so I'd like to tell you a little bit about myself.

First of all, let's get a few things out in the open. I consider myself to be a spiritual person. But that does not mean that I am a perfect person. I have plenty of faults. If I'm just hanging out with friends, I can swear like a sailor, I enjoy a good dirty joke, and if the truth be told, I don't get along with my mother-in-law. From the moment I first got together with her son, in fact, she's been a real rock in my underwear. A real pickle-puss. But don't get me started. Aside from the usual number of human flaws, I think I'm pretty easy to get along with. Just your average Jersey girl who talks to the dead.

I'm a pretty upfront person, but I haven't always been open about that last bit. I've accepted it now, sort of grown into it, but especially when I was younger that's the last thing I'd want anyone to know about me. I haven't been public all that long—only for the past ten years, and that took a lot of prodding (I'll say more about that later)—but now that I realize how important it is, I've become a lot more willing to talk about this ability and the incredible things I've learned from it.

As soon as I made the decision to go public with my unusual

talent, the questions came in full force. There have been serious questions, silly questions, sad questions, snide questions. I answered them truthfully, patiently . . . and *repeatedly*. This book is an attempt to answer all of the questions I have been asked over the years, and finally put an end to that one question I am asked most: When are you going to write a book?

In the past I would respond as any severely dyslexic girl who didn't know how to type would—I changed the subject. But after a while I realized it might be easier to just write the damn book than to keep fielding the damn question.

Within these pages I am going to be as upfront and open as possible. I will try to keep the cursing and mentions of my mother-in-law problem to a minimum. But you should know that it may come up from time to time. Sometimes even a rock in the underwear can be a good teacher—even if the lesson is that you can't please everyone! I hope I can bring some understanding to the subject of what happens to us all when we pass over from the land of the living to the Other Side. I hope some of what you'll find in these pages may be comforting to you. And if I can make someone smile, so much the better!

What is the difference between a medium and a psychic?

A medium is a psychic, but a psychic is not necessarily a medium. Someone who is just psychic can give you a prediction, but they can't tell you where or who they got it from. I (and other true mediums) not only can tell you what is going on and what will happen, but we can tell you who on the Other Side is bringing the message. I'm the whole package, baby!

When did you first start talking with dead people?

I can't say exactly, but certainly it was when I was a small girl. It wasn't really having a conversation, I just *knew* something. I understood so little at that time, I had no one to explain to me what this "knowing" was. One of my very earliest memories of this was walking home one day when I was about nine years old (this wasn't the first, but one that I strongly recall) and "realizing" that my older brother was going to be taken from us at an early age. As I was walking into my backyard, I "heard" the Other Side (I didn't know at the time that's who was communicating with me) tell me this. I can't recall the exact words I heard. I'm not even sure it was a full sentence. Nevertheless, I knew what they meant, and I remember it like it was yesterday.

Other messages like this one came to me at other times. I was told, for example, that I would never in this lifetime have children of my own. I was also told that in a past lifetime my soul had been married to my father's soul—one of the reasons, I'm sure, why I completely adored my father in this lifetime. The effect of these messages, for me, was one of grounding me. Even if I didn't like what I'd been told, even if, like anyone would, I fought against losing my brother and against whatever it was that decided I would not have children, the fact that I'd been told these things in advance eventually helped me gain perspective.

When did you first tell someone about the things you "knew"?

I don't think it even dawned on me to talk about these things. I guess when you're young, you don't really know what's normal to know or not know. But I remember one event that my mother has said was the first time she was aware that anything special was going on with me. I was just a small child playing outside in the backyard. My mother recalls that I came into the kitchen and declared that my uncle Jerry's leg was all bloody. My mother was shocked that I would say such a thing, and told me to go back outside to play. A short time later, our kitchen phone rang and my mother got the news that her brother Jerry had been in a motorcycle accident and they were going to amputate his leg. Fortunately, the doctors were able to save his leg, but my mother was never the same! She didn't know what to make of what I had told her and at the time she was really frightened.

When my father came home from work that night, my mother told him the story. As my mother tells it, he just sat there without any expression. Finally he said, "Well, looks like Pop was right. He said she had the gift."

My grandfather had been a gifted medium. He crossed over when I was very young so I don't really remember him from this side. But we're in contact now and I've gotten to know him from the Other Side. Maybe now is a good time to say that even though my grandfather said I had "the gift" I'm not really comfortable with that term. I would never say that about myself. To me, it kind of sounds pretentious to say, *my gift*. I think of it more as an ability, the way everyone has different abilities. But sometimes in this book I may use the term *gift* just because it's shorter and I tend to talk fast.

Why does mediumship run in families?

I believe that it is just like any other talent that seems to run in families, like the ability to draw and paint, or having a good ear for music and being able to sing or play an instrument. We don't really question that, it's almost expected: "Well of course she can sing—her mother was a music teacher!" Nobody would think it the least bit weird if Picasso had a son who was a painter. But, like any other talent, there's also a choice that goes along with it. Maybe everyone in your family was a teacher—they just had a knack for communicating ideas, and maybe you also have this knack. But you can't see yourself in a classroom with kids all day long, your whole life. You might choose to use that talent in another way. Or you might decide that that's not the most important thing to you, there's something else you'd rather do. You still have the talent, but you don't have to use it at all. That's our free will.

Right now, my brother Bobby and sister-in-law Choi's little girl, my niece Bobbie Concetta—she's six years old and a real sweetheart!—has the ability I have and that my grandfather had. She has spoken about people who are on the Other Side and has described a lot of things about her past lives. One time, when she and her mother were walking by a church, she pointed to a statue of a woman with clearly Caucasian features and said, "That's the way my last mommy looked." Being my sister-in-law, Choi knows all about this kind of thing and showed no fear, maybe just curiosity. So there is a strong likelihood that with this support Bobbie Concetta will retain the ability she has now. Is Bobbie Concetta currently giving readings to her little friends? No. And she may never do what I'm doing. It's up to her. She'll have to decide for herself.

How did being psychic affect you growing up?

I don't remember feeling different from the other kids in my neighborhood. I basically had the same interests as other girls my age—the normal stuff of dances and boys, tests and grades (and not usually *good* grades), and the occasional teacher who was not fond of me, usually because I talked too much in class. (Also, I'm deaf in one ear so I sometimes don't know how loud I am and the principal's secretary used to call me Microphone Mouth, which really hurt my feelings.) But I remember knowing things that I couldn't explain. For example, I was able to choose long-lasting friends for my lifetime. I just thought that I had gotten lucky where friends were concerned, but somehow I knew that a little girl in my class, Cornelia, who we all call Mushy, would be a best friend for life. We were complete opposites—Mushy was pretty and smart; I was the class clown. We didn't even *like* each other. But the Other Side told me that we'd be friends, and Mushy and I have been best friends from grade school to today.

The Other Side was also involved in how I treated others and in helping me develop self-confidence. I never felt like a particularly intelligent person. I had dyslexia and as a result I always had trouble with numbers. When I was young, dyslexia was not often diagnosed so my teachers assumed I wasn't trying or just wasn't good in math, and I ended up feeling stupid. But at the same time I was getting messages from "them" that were very encouraging and helped me to feel better about myself. They also urged me to do the right thing where other people were concerned, to not tease or pick on someone who was weaker, and to stand up for the underdog. I'm not patting myself on the back here—just explaining how, along with my parents, the Other Side made it clear to me how bad it was to take part in hurting anyone else's feelings and the difference between right and wrong.

Being psychic did sometimes get me into some hot water. There were certain teachers who felt I was a sneak because I knew things that I should not have known—I even knew things that I didn't understand! I remember when I was around eleven or twelve years old I would see visions around some of the teachers I had—just little scenes that told me something about them. In one case, there was this teacher who would let kids smoke and not report them so they would think he was cool, but I could tell from the images I saw that he was not on the up and up, so I avoided him and later I heard that he had been improperly involved with at least one student. In another case, I saw images around two of my teachers—my gym teacher and the home ec teacher—of them together, lying in bed together. I was young, I had no idea about lesbian relationships, and no clue whatsoever about sex of any kind—I was so naïve! This image didn't register to me as anything "secret," just maybe like they were good friends having a sleepover. Innocently, I told one of my friends that I knew that these two teachers slept together—I didn't even know what it meant. The teacher whose class we were in said, "Concetta, would you like to come up here and tell the whole class what you're talking about?" I didn't want to, but the kid I had told this story to didn't mind getting up and repeating what I'd said. Next thing you know, I was sent home from school and I didn't even know what I was in trouble for. My mother came and picked me up. She said, "Want to go get some ice cream?" This was not at all what I was expecting! When my friends got in trouble at school, they were always worried about how their parents would react, and I, too, tried to think how I'd present my story to my mother. How could I explain to her what I didn't even understand myself? But I was lucky. I never had to explain to her; somehow she always seemed to just know.

I don't mean to suggest that I was always innocent. Quite the contrary. I enjoyed tempting authority. Over time I got smarter about it and used my ability more carefully—I could outfox the foxes, my teachers, and was not caught. But all this time I was just playing with my ability and I really had no idea how I knew the things I knew. That all changed when I was sixteen.

One night, I woke up to hear voices speaking to me. I smelled fresh flowers and I could hear voices all around me. I sat up in bed, looking around, trying to see everything in my room to understand where all the voices could be coming from. My mind wanted to make normal sense of it all. Even though I was not threatened, I was afraid.

The voices were telling me that I was to share my special ability, that I had chosen this ability to learn many lessons, but, most important, I was here to help people understand about death. I didn't know what to make of any of this. I was untrained, and I thought I might be insane. I screamed for the one person I knew would protect me, and my father came running with my mother close behind him.

The moment my father turned on the light, the spirits were gone. I struggled to tell my parents what had happened. I begged them to listen and insisted that it was not a dream. To my surprise, they looked at each other and led me out of my room to their bedroom. We all sat on their bed and my father said, "We know." It was a long story and a long night.

How did your parents help you to deal with this ability?

At that time, my parents discussed the situation and made the decision not to say anything to me until I was old enough to understand. My mother was especially concerned for me as she had been raised in an orphanage and knew all too well that being *different* could mean being punished.

My father was already experienced with this because his father had the ability and he knew how his father had helped a lot of people in their neighborhood, bringing them comfort and understanding about death. He wasn't frightened, so right away that helped me. He talked with me about it, and made it seem *normal*, even if somewhat special. My mother may have been a little freaked out at first, but she trusted my father, and so pretty much followed his lead. And both my parents always made sure that I felt loved and safe. They didn't treat me like I was weird in any way.

Did you begin doing readings as soon as you began to understand your gift?

Not at all. I was sixteen and wanted to be normal, to be like everyone else. At the time I was certain that I didn't want this gift. My father told me that if I didn't want to hear Them, all I had to do was envision myself surrounded by the white light of God and simply say, "In the name of God, be gone." I couldn't believe it was that easy, but it was. The voices went away. Completely. For four years.

After the spirits left me, some time later, it got to the point where I was actually thinking that maybe I'd imagined the things I'd experienced. My experiences were beginning to seem unreal to me, and eventually I just wanted to know the truth.

At first I didn't want to talk about it at all. But soon I became curious and began to go see other psychics to see if they could explain what was happening to me. I saw a bunch of them because each time I didn't really trust what they said (and definitely some of them are what I call boardwalk psychics, completely phony, just there to take your money). I wondered sometimes if I'd imagined everything, if I was sick somehow, like something was wrong with my mind, or if what I'd experienced had even happened at all. Over the next eight years I searched and sought to understand. I discussed it with my father and he explained that one of my lessons was about choices and consequences. I didn't have to take the gift, but that choice would have a consequence, just as accepting it would. During this time, I was flirting with the idea of wishing it back. It wasn't until I was twenty-four, when I met a man named Alfonse Demino through an associate at work, that I got the push I needed.

Meeting Al was strange in itself because the invitation came from a girl at work whom I didn't even know well. She said that friends of her parents knew me and wanted to see me, and she invited me to her parents' house. I thought this was weird, but didn't have any particular reason to feel nervous about it so I asked my friend Terry if she wanted to come with me. Terry didn't have a car so we were going to take mine. But the day we were to go, my car got hit while it was parked and the side got smooshed in so we couldn't take it. The next week, that side was fixed and I went to get my car again and the *other side* had been smooshed by a snow plow! Finally, the third week we got on our way. I knew exactly where we were going, but somehow Terry and I got completely lost and we didn't find our way to the house for two hours. By the time we arrived, Al and his wife were just leaving. I was apologizing like crazy and Al said, "Don't worry about it. I understand. Someone doesn't want us to meet. We have to go now because we have a long drive home, but just come back next week."

After four tries, we all finally got together the following week. Al and his wife seemed like relatives to me. We had a lovely night of cake and coffee before Al turned to me and said, "Concetta, They told me about you. They say that you refused the gift and They want me to help you understand." To say I was flabbergasted would be an understatement. I had never mentioned anything about being psychic to anyone at work. Al told me that I had nothing to be afraid of because I was protected (even when my car got smooshed, I was never in it). I was in control of it at all times. I just needed to trust Them and They would help me.

But first we had to get rid of whoever it was who had been

trying to keep Al and me from meeting. He asked our hostess to find a candle. She went through some drawers and finally came up with a little stub of a candle, about two inches high—I'm not even sure what she was saving it for, it was so small. Al had all of us sit in a circle and hold hands and he lit the candle. As we watched it, the flame leaped up about two feet high, like a blow-torch, then went back down, then leaped up again, then again. I've never seen a candle flame behave like this, before or since. I'm just glad Terry was there to witness it with me. After we were done with this Al said that whatever spirit it was who'd been making the trouble wouldn't be doing it anymore.

I began visiting with Al regularly. He'd tell me things about living with this kind of ability and he suggested some books to read. Al told me that he had worked and studied with someone named Hans Byer (I'm not sure about the spelling of this name), who he said was a famous medium in Europe. I was curious about who Byer was, and when I later learned about Edgar Cayce, I thought that probably Byer might have been on par with him (but Google didn't exist in those days), but to be honest, I was most curious to know how Al had known about *me!*

During one of our weekly visits, Al told me he would visit me at my job the following day. I knew he lived far away, but I didn't question it. The next day I was sitting at my desk, busy with a pile of papers. Terry was right there next to me. As I turned to type a letter, I felt this amazing breeze go by my face. I sat in a small, stuffy cubicle with hardly any air, never mind a breeze—but the breeze was undeniable. I looked up and everything seemed to be going in slow motion. Terry's and my eyes met and I knew she was feeling the same thing. I moved my head and went to lift my hand to my face. I felt the breeze, then, go through my whole body. I heard Al's voice clearly say, "I told you I would visit." It seemed like the whole thing took ten minutes but it was probably only ten seconds. Before I could even speak, Terry said, "Don't say anything! Just write on a piece of paper what you think just happened." She and I both grabbed paper and pen and wrote down our experiences. When we compared, we'd written almost exactly the same thing, word for word. I made a note of the day and time, Thursday, 2:20 p.m., and told no one what had happened. The following week when I saw Al, the first thing he said to me was "Thursday, 2:20 in the afternoon." I showed him the small piece of paper with that written on it, and from that moment began to trust the Other Side and myself.

When I met Al, I began to think, "Maybe I've given up something that might benefit me." It was a selfish thought, like, maybe having this ability could help me get a better job or help me find my true love. I had no idea that this might be more of a calling or life's work.

When I asked the ability to come back to me, it didn't happen right away. I began taking a meditation course and asked for help from Them. I asked protection from God and really put it all in His hands. Slowly, I began to see proof of Their presence around me. They played jokes on me—I would turn off the lights and They would turn them back on. I would walk out of the bathroom and They would turn the faucet on full blast. Eventually, the voices came back, too.

How did you "come out," so to speak, as a medium?

For quite a while I still wanted to keep it all a secret. I was always hesitant to tell people about my ability, mostly because of the negative reactions of unbelievers. There is, even now, a lot of misunderstanding surrounding what I do, and I didn't want to subject myself or my family to any kind of attack—verbal or otherwise. So for the first forty years of my life, I kept a low profile. So low, I didn't even tell my husband!

I know that sounds strange, and maybe even unethical to not reveal something like that to the person you're sharing your life with. But when I began dating John, I learned pretty quickly that he did not believe in God or anything "supernatural." John is a very concrete, real world kind of guy. He builds houses, he deals with lumber and tools, and—literally—concrete. He believes in the things he can touch or hold in his hands. "Ghosts" don't really fit into that category. I had no idea back then what a huge part of my life being psychic would become. I thought of it as just a small part of who I was, and so made the decision not to say anything about it. It's ironic, really because *They* had already told me that John was "the one," so I didn't want John to know about *Them* because I didn't want to blow it with him! You have to admit, it's a pretty unusual position to be in. Then, after we married, I already wasn't getting along so great with John's family. The last thing I needed was to introduce the subject over Thanksgiving dinner, like maybe tell my mother-in-law that *her* mother-in-law was sending her tips to improve her stuffing from beyond the grave. *I don't think so.* I kept my mouth shut.

The trouble was that in my old neighborhood in Montville, New Jersey, everyone knew about my ability. So whenever a loved one died, I'd get a call: "Concetta, can you come and let us know that he (or she) arrived safely? We want to be sure they're okay." Or we would be at some family gathering and one of my cousins would whisper to me that someone wanted a reading. And without telling John where I was going, I just went. To be honest, in the early days of our marriage, things were pretty difficult, most of it due to family strains. But we were trying to keep it together, and had agreed to go to counseling—our therapist was a former nun. So in one of our sessions, John said, "She's always whispering with other people, always keeping secrets." The therapist said, "Concetta, what are you whispering about?" I said, "Nothing." I didn't know what to say, even though it was very clear to me that John thought the whispering was about another man, that I was having an affair. As bad as I knew that was, at the time, it seemed like saying I was talking to dead people would be even worse.

But along with our joint sessions, we also had one-on-one sessions with the therapist and she wasn't about to let this go. As soon as she had me alone she asked me again what I was whispering about, and I told her. She asked me, "Do you see anyone around me?" I said yes, so she asked me to tell her what I saw and heard. When I did, she seemed pretty blown away. In our next joint session, she said, "John, Concetta has something to tell you." She said, "In my reading and research I have learned that these things are possible, and Concetta has single-handedly convinced me that this is real." So I had to come clean.

It was much better than having my husband think I was sneaking around on him, even if it didn't feel like it at first. But still, I wasn't hanging out a shingle.

How did your husband react to the news that you talk to the dead?

It really was not easy for John. When he married me, he had no idea that this was part of the deal—it wasn't what he signed up for. And he didn't really understand it at all. In John's world, dead people were in the same category as elves. I remember when I first told him, in our therapy session, he said, "Oh great. Now besides worrying about *you* I have to worry about *little people?*" Once it began to sink in, I think he was pretty uneasy. He wasn't sure where all this would go or what it would mean in our lives and our marriage. I have to give John a tremendous amount of credit. This went completely against his worldview, but he never tried to stop me and what I was doing, and he never placed demands on me.

If I had to do it all over again, I'd certainly be more open. But realize it's a different world now. Back then might as well have been the 1600s instead of the 1980s! There were no TV shows featuring psychics or mediums, and certainly none that featured them so favorably! I'm relieved for those being born with the gift that nowadays it's not such a big deal to say to your fiancé, "Uh, honey . . . what I do goes just a teeny tiny bit beyond intuition." And you never know, they might have their own secret or superpower to reveal!

Was there one event that made you go public?

What finally made me go public was the death of my brother Harold in 1991. Harold's death was the first time I had ever lost someone I had known and loved so deeply. Before, I really couldn't understand what everyone got out of it, to have me describe their loved one on the Other Side and pass along a message or two—most of them incredibly mundane and seemingly unimportant. Now I finally understood. I was devastated to lose Harold. He was thirty-eight when he passed away. He had been fighting AIDS for six years and at the end of his fight he carried only eighty pounds on his formerly fit six-foot-two frame. He looked so tired and so sickly and we all knew it was his time to go. He could not stay here any longer. I had been told that Harold would cross over at an early age and I understood he would be happier on the Other Side, but that didn't make it any easier to see him go. I knew it was selfish—and I knew I'd get to talk with him again—but I still wanted him here with me. For the first time I understood the pain we associate with death on this side. I had been talking to the dead almost all my life, but before they were just spirits that I didn't know, and to be honest, at times I found them to be nuisances! I didn't always want to hear these voices, but now there was one voice in particular that I was desperate to hear. And it didn't come.

For months I waited to hear Harold's voice and I was crushed and confused as to why he wasn't coming through to speak to me. But one cold December night I was sleeping in the guest bedroom—John had the flu and I did *not* want to catch it—and suddenly the bed was shaking off the floor. At first I thought it was an earthquake—not too common in New Jersey, but I was half asleep—then I noticed that nothing else in the room was moving. I was scared out of my mind! Until I heard my big brother's laugh. "Hey Con," he called out, "it's me!" He was still laughing (he thought he was *so* funny) and I cried out, "Harold!? You jerk! Where have you been?" He didn't answer me that night and he didn't stay long, but after that he started to come through quite often and he would always tell me, "Con, *tell* them. Tell the world what you hear. We need you to. And they need you on that side, too." I was still nervous about what might happen, but I couldn't say no to my brother. I told him I couldn't make any promises about how it would turn out, but I said, "Okay, buddy. I'll try."

For about five years I just "dabbled," but Harold kept pushing me and also strongly suggesting that I should move to the country, which sounded like a wonderful idea. I'm a country girl at heart. I grew up in Montville, which at that time was all country roads and barns; there was a cow pasture right across the street from my school. The smell of cow manure is like roses to me! John and I had been living about forty-five minutes from Montville (or half an hour, the way I drive) in West Orange, which was way more populated. All the Oranges are urban/suburban and I was always getting lost—there are Orange, East Orange, West Orange, South Orange—I hated all those Oranges! Also, John had relatives on every corner and I was suffocating. We couldn't make the move right away, but in 1996 when the kids graduated high school (John has a daughter and son from his first marriage and I think of them as my own) we made the move to the woods of Boonton, New Jersey. I could finally breathe and almost immediately I began to formally take clients.

Much to my shock and surprise, it was a kind of overnight success story. I was instantly booked for months in advance. Then it happened that James Van Praagh was doing this study to find "real" psychics. He had someone in the area who was going to see various psychics and report back to him which were legitimate. He had a reading with me and I guess I got a good report. Next thing you know, I was getting referrals from James. One person he sent was movie producer Jon Cornick, with whom I've become good friends. Jon passed my name to Federico Castelluccio of *The Sopranos*. He had a reading and next thing I knew, Edie Falco and Vincent Curatola were making appointments. When celebrities started to come all the way out to the sticks to have readings I had to admit that Harold was right.

Ten years after my brother's death, my father, Manny, crossed over. It wasn't long after that that I had my first big show. I was very nervous—even though I'm a total ham I had never had a crowd that big come to see *me*! My best friend, Mushy, was there with me acting as master of ceremonies and when she saw the blank look on my face as I approached the audience I know she was thinking: Oh. My. God.

I started out very slow, nervous, and choppy. But as I began to talk I suddenly was flooded with energy. It was almost like an old LP record being started up with the needle down—dragging at first, but finally getting up to speed and playing normally. But then getting switched to 78! Well, not quite. But to say that I soon felt extremely comfortable as the center of attention would be an understatement. I was in my element.

Later, going home in the car, Mushy said to me, "Your father is very proud of you." Then she looked at me and said, "I don't know why I said that!" But I knew. My father was with me the whole time. That night as I lay in bed, my father came to me and told me in person, "I'm so proud of you." He leaned down and kissed me. I actually felt the pressure of his lips on mine. And then I was 100 percent sure that I was doing the right thing.

When you meet new people do you always introduce yourself as a medium?

Absolutely not. I always think that if I say that I am a medium, they are going to say, "No, honey, you're a large!"

Sometimes I experience déjà vu or feel as if I predicted events that came to pass, does this mean that I am psychic? How can I know if my abilities are ordinary or extraordinary?

Well, it's probably different for each person, but I think it would be self-evident, a matter of clarity of detail instead of just impressions of things. If you do hear voices, or rather fully articulated thoughts that don't seem to be your own, that would be a big clue. Or if you see visions or ghosts. Everyone *can*, but for most it's not a common occurrence. I'm not sure if there is any place where you can actually go to be tested these days. Thirty years ago, in the 1970s, I went with a guy I was dating to the Edgar Cayce Foundation (also known as the ARE—Association for Research and Enlightenment). Edgar Cayce was a photographer who was psychic and used to go into trances and diagnose people's health problems and prescribe cures for them, when he had no medical background or experience in his conscious waking state. His cures really worked and people began to take them down, as well as to transcribe things he said in his trance state (he was nicknamed "the Sleeping Prophet"), and all of these thousands of pages of transcriptions are archived at the ARE in Virginia Beach, Virginia. In any case, my boyfriend knew someone there so we went. In those days, you could take a little tour of the place and they'd give you a little ESP (extrasensory perception) test as part of the tour. So we did that, but then I was taken "backstage" as it were for real testing. To be honest, it was so long ago, I don't remember in great detail what all the tests were. I only recall that they started out with very simple stuff at first, I suppose to gauge whether they were wasting their time. Then the tests became more complicated—identifying pictures of things that weren't in the same room with me and that kind of thing. To give you an idea, let's say we were sitting together in the kitchen and we heard a car pull up in the driveway out in front of the house. I might say to you, "Who do you think just pulled in?" You're at my house, not your own, so you really don't have a clue, but you might get a psychic impression that it was so-and-so. That's along the lines of what those tests were like. By the end of it all, the professionals at the ARE had determined that my abilities were real and that I would be classified a *clairesentient*, since I got messages in a combination of ways—part seeing images, part hearing, part feeling, and so on.

What happens to us when we die?

People have fears. They've heard about going into the Light and want to know, does it hurt walking into the Light? Do we lose our memories? Is everything there that we had before?

What I've heard from the souls on the Other Side is that when we die we leave either through our feet or the top of the head. On this side I've heard of the "silver cord" that supposedly attaches us to life here, but no one from over there has ever mentioned this to me. It's hard to describe exactly how we are moving—it's a bit like floating, a bit like walking, a bit like flying, it's a "gravitating" toward the Light. There's a feeling of anticipation—maybe a little fear, but more anticipation.

Nothing at all is forgotten. In fact, whereas now we can remember only some highlights of our past, over there we remember every single moment and detail. Everything we knew, loved, or experienced.

When we die, within *seconds* of entering the Light we experience a knowing. We get a fast-forward review of our lives and see the whole domino effect of all of our actions. We feel everything we made someone else feel—the joy, the hurt. We see and understand the whole domino effect of all our actions and of every interaction we had with anyone. And we know and understand what our purpose was in this lifetime.

There's a period of transition, a time we get to reflect on our lives—I don't feel that this is standardized in any way; it's different from individual to individual. For many there may be a necessary period of healing any physical or emotional issues, especially forgiving ourselves for anything we did while living that we don't feel proud of, that may have hurt someone, before we are able to interact with this side, the living, again. At all times we are given help in healing what we "shoulda woulda coulda" done in our lives here. Sometimes there is sadness at what we wish we could have done differently. We're encouraged to heal any anger or guilt. But there is also what we would think of as physical healing—even though it's not really physical, it's spiritual. I can't tell you how often people who had been sick when they died, maybe even have been missing parts of their bodies, have told me in spirit that they are completely healed and healthy, and completely whole. Someone who may have had great difficulty walking or even standing on this side at the end of her life will tell me that over there she is dancing.

The true beauty of the Light is that it is total harmony. Here, we can spend a lifetime in the dark. We don't know what we are doing or the effect we are having. But when we get over there, we get a clear view of what *this* side is all about.

Is there a heaven?

Yes, the Other Side is heaven. I don't usually use that term. I'm more likely to say *paradise* or just *the Other Side*. Until we go back it's very hard for us to even imagine it, it's more miraculous than anything we can make, believe, perform, or create on this side. I just don't think the human mind has the capacity to grasp it, even though at our deepest core we do indeed remember it.

When we cross over is there really a "God" to meet?

There is, absolutely a God, and we do meet Him. But it is not like meeting the king or the president. God is not a separate entity we are introduced to and shake hands with and say, "How wonderful to meet you, I've heard so much about you!" God is *all* and when we cross we go from being a piece of God to being one with God, so it's more joining with God than meeting God. God is pure loving energy. The very Light that we go into as we cross is God. As the old prayer goes, God is the Power and the Glory. For ever and ever, till eternity, to infinity. We can't possibly imagine or describe all that God is. But our deepest consciousness knows God, and the miracle is that we all will get the chance to go home and join God.

Wait, wait, wait—are you saying definitively that God is a He?

No, God is neither He nor She. Nor It. Obviously calling God He is just for convenience's sake, because of the limits of our language. Even though spirits will present themselves to me as one gender or the other, it's only so that I can relay their message to someone on this side in a way that person will relate to and understand. When we cross we are no gender. We are pure energy and one with God. God is All That. And more.

What do we look like when we die?

We no longer have any physical appearance. We're pure energy. When I'm doing a reading, the dead do have ways of showing me some appearance that allows me to describe them to their loved one on this side, but to be honest, I don't know how they do that.

What is there to do on the Other Side?

There are so many dimensions, we have the choice of any kind of beauty we wish to experience. Whatever we loved is there—how could it be paradise otherwise? If we liked baseball on this side, we might choose to spend most of our time in a big beautiful baseball park, watching or playing our favorite game. If we liked to fish we can choose to be on a gorgeous, sparkling lake. If we liked the mountains, we could go skiing for as long as we want. If we liked music, we might be in a wonderful music hall. These dimensions are all created by God.

I was doing a reading for this woman once and I said, "Your husband is there with so-and-so and they are playing checkers." She said, "No, they always played backgammon together." Okay, I'm not perfect—I always say this—but the point is that the game they enjoyed on this side, they still were playing on that side. I've had spirits tell me they are still enjoying their weekly card games, whatever!

Can you explain what a near-death experience is about?

In most cases a near-death experience (NDE) is precipitated by some traumatic event such as an accident or a serious illness, a situation in which the physical body could be permanently put out of commission. But there are some individuals, very deeply spiritual or mystical people, who through their spiritual practice of meditation can also have this experience, or one with very similar elements, without the body being harmed.

What happens is that the soul lifts out of the physical body and travels through a tunnel of light that normally would be our "Last Exit to Brooklyn," so to speak, our passage to the Other Side, where we'd stay until it's time for us to reincarnate again. The same thing happens as would happen upon death—the person is greeted by loved ones who have already crossed, they will have a life review, they may get a tour of some kind or be given a class of some kind from a spiritual Master that they are told to remember. It's so beautiful and peaceful there that very often, I've heard, the person does not want to return to the body, but somebody on the Other Side will tell them that it's not their time. They have to go back.

On this side, while the soul is out of the body, if the person is under medical care, it's very common that he or she will actually be pronounced dead—there will be no vital signs. But when the soul reenters the body: "Surprise, surprise!"

Is an NDE just something that accidentally happens? Or is there a reason that certain people are chosen to "almost die"?

I think that having a near-death experience is really a gift from God. The truth is that we are in constant contact with God. Always. But our awareness of this flits in and out. Having an NDE heightens that awareness. If a person is off the track in his life, it can be a wake-up call that he needs to get his wheels realigned and get back on the right road.

Sometimes it's not the case that the person was messing up. Maybe the Masters on the Other Side see him as someone with potential to facilitate a needed change over here. A person might be given messages that are for the larger world, or be given a specific mission that he is to accomplish with the time he has left in this world.

What about someone in a coma? Are they trying to cross? Can or do they stay here for us?

A person in a coma is literally between heaven and earth. In some cases, it may really be their time to cross; in other cases, they may revive naturally. I do believe that initially when someone is in a coma she is in a deep sleep and doesn't realize she could leave her body. However, if someone is in a coma for many months or years, I don't believe that he just lies there sleeping. I believe that his soul can and does leave his body. How it does this, I really don't know, but I equate it with the ability to experience astral travel. And, too, some are likely having NDEs.

There's no single answer to this; it's individual. Some probably are very much wanting to cross, and it's their time to go. At times, we keep them here medically because we now know how to keep the body going with our technology. I personally do not believe in life support. I don't believe that we have the right to keep someone here who, naturally, would cross. That is just my belief, but it does not mean that I am right; it's simply how I feel about that issue.

The main reason, I believe, that people in comas do not cross is simply fear. They may have fear of the crossing itself. They're at an intersection and probably have fear of the unknown, they don't know if crossing will mean that they cease to exist in any way. They may fear that in going, someone they leave behind will be hurt. They need to make a choice and they're afraid of making the *wrong* choice; they're stuck. I don't think it's the energy of *our* wanting them here that literally holds them. I think it's the energy of their *own* fears about that that does so.

Have you ever done a reading where you heard from someone who technically was still living?

No, not exactly. But I think you may be referring to someone who is, as we might put it, at death's door. Usually in cases like that, I'm not hearing from that person but from other spirits that have already crossed. They may be telling me that this person will be joining them soon, that they are getting ready to call him. That person might even be seeing the spirits of his family who are waiting to receive him. Like someone in a coma, he may be lingering, not sure about going, maybe having some fears. But it's his time. In any case, I'm not talking *with* that person; I'm hearing *about* that person.

If it's someone's time, can they decide not to go?

I believe they can decline. But I doubt that this could continue on and on. So far, we have not earned eternal life in the flesh (and I'm not sure that would be such a prize to win, anyway, even though I know some see that as a goal). I think there would have to be a good reason for someone to be able to stay once they've been called. From everything I've heard, I believe that when we are called, there is nothing we'd like more than to go. It's true that we might linger if we think someone here will be hurt by our leaving, but almost always we want to go. I can't tell you how many times I've heard in a reading that hearing a loved one say to them "It's okay to go" made all the difference. They are so grateful for that.

How is it decided who will greet us on the Other Side?

I can't give a definitive answer here, like a formula, but it has to do with those we've loved and lost, as well as the spirit Masters (kind of like caseworkers) who have been involved with our lives while we are here. It will always be a group of souls bringing us back home. If, for example, someone has been told in a reading that her husband will be coming to get her when it's her time, that soul will be there, but he won't be alone. He'll be with a host of others. We may think that we'll "only have eyes" for that one individual soul when we cross, but what happens is that as soon as we enter the Light and that knowing comes over us, we will recognize all the other souls who are with that one. We'll recognize even souls that we didn't know, this time, on earth, but knew before in other lives.

Do the dead know things about our pasts that they couldn't have known while they were alive?

They know everything. They are like God. When they cross over they become omniscient, all knowing—they know all of our thoughts and impulses. Even things they didn't understand before, they now see clearly. It is revealed to them why things happened exactly the way they did.

Once we cross we completely understand, for example, why our mates behaved the way they did, what their mission was, how it related to ours, everything behind anything that didn't make sense to us before. Any skeletons in the family closet that might have been hidden from us, we will know about. I recall a reading I was doing for a woman and her son came through, I don't recall if I was told the circumstances, but he crossed before his mother. He told his mother that he knew that the person he'd always known here as his uncle was really his father. But he wasn't accusing his mom. He told her he understood why she couldn't say anything about it, why she'd had to keep this hidden, what it would have done to their family if anyone had known it.

Do the dead judge the living?

They don't judge at all—we are the ones who make judgments, even though it isn't our place to do so. On the Other Side, there is no room for anything other than complete love, forgiveness, and joy. Judgment does not have a place there at all.

How does religion work on the Other Side?

Once we cross over there are not different religions. You don't get to the Other Side and see eighteen desks and a dispatcher directing you: "Muslims to the left, Jews to the right, Catholics down the hall, second door to the right." We are all the same when we get to the Other Side. We are all one. There's not a dozen or two dozen different heavens we go to. It's all the same place. What do you think? If I'm doing a reading for Mr. Goldberg I get an operator? "Just a minute, Miss, while I connect you with the Jewish heaven." No. It's the same place for you, for me, for people of every color, creed, or religion.

God created these religions—and really, *all* our differences—because he wanted to show us to love one another *despite* our differences. And that's not how it worked out, so far. I'm sure God is very sad about that. There's an ad I really like on TV. I think it's for the Church of Jesus Christ of Latter-Day Saints, the Mormons. The scene is inside a church and first you see this gay couple sitting in the pew together, and down at the bottom of the screen is a button and a big hand comes in and pushes the button and the couple goes flying out of the church. Then you see an old homeless woman come in and sit down and again the hand comes in and hits the button and she goes flying out of the church. Then you see a biracial couple come in with a cute little baby and here comes the hand again, hitting the ejector button, and the whole family goes flying. And then there's the message: God does not reject anybody. *That* is the real truth. God does not reject *anybody*. I like this ad because it makes me feel like maybe the world is finally waking up, beginning to change, becoming more accepting. Do I care if there's someone of every race, class, and sexual orientation at my barbecue? Does that hurt me? The only one who would be bothered by that is someone in a white hood and sheet, and they are definitely *not* welcome at chez Bertoldi!

Do we worship God on the Other Side?

No. We don't worship God. But we both love God and are God. When we are here we are limited, we are only a piece of God. But over there, we are united as one unlimited "body of God," for lack of a better way to put it.

Does everyone go into the Light?

No. Murderers are not invited to the party. Evil does not go into the Light. Hitler, Charles Manson, Ted Bundy, and the like are not going to be there, which I am happy about since I don't think I ever want to be at the same party with Hitler. I can carry on a conversation with most people, but I'd probably have a bit of a problem with someone like that.

Each of us has a reckoning at the end of our lives and will have to answer for all our actions, and they will, too, but not in the same place. Someone like O.J. Simpson, who thinks he got away with murder, will have another reckoning. I looked at the facts of that case as a person, and I listened to the dead as a medium, and I believe that he is guilty, and though he may think he got away with his crime, I assure you he did not. From all I know or have heard it is my belief that what we think of as hell is not a hot, fiery place where the evil burn forever. It's completely without light of any kind, very cold and very dark. Completely without love. To be honest, I don't have a complete understanding of this realm because I don't deal in that.

Do you believe there is such a thing as pure evil?

Yes, I really do. What we call the devil, or an evil spirit, really does exist. Just as there is positive, there is also negative—this is a world of duality and you can't have one without the other. But I also believe that the good is more powerful than the evil. If you think about it, you can bring one small candle into a dark room and it's not dark anymore. But darkness can't make a candle not light. The light can eliminate the dark, but the dark can't eliminate the light.

If people have had a violent crossing, for instance, if they were victims of murder, are they heartbroken in heaven or do they find peace?

On the Other Side They do find peace. They *are* peace. They *are* love. There may be some initial anger over having their lives cut short, not getting to do what they incarnated to do. But once They are given understanding, that feeling passes away very quickly. Anger and heartbreak are not at all the norm on the Other Side. We have to bear in mind also that maybe They did know that was part of the plan for them, part of what They agreed to before coming. We can't know that. I have done readings, for example, where someone who died in the attacks on the World Trade Center has come through, and he or she expressed no anger at all. They knew they had made a sacrifice and there would be change of some kind because of that.

When we think of anger and heartbreak, we're thinking in terms of the flesh. We might think, on this side, Man, that really sucks to be killed. We see it as the loss of life, the loss of the body, the loss of what we see as volition. We might compare being killed to being imprisoned for life, stuck in a cell with no hope of getting out, and seeing our whole life expire day by day without our being able to make anything of it. But in fact, even if it was not what they thought they wanted, in death they are liberated. In spirit, they are unlimited. They haven't lost us; they're still with us. So it's an entirely different perspective.

If someone is killed violently, does he experience the trauma of his assault or is he whisked out of his body somehow so he doesn't suffer?

Oh, definitely he is immediately whisked from his body and gathered up by a group of souls and taken to a place of intense, perfect love. The souls immediately help that person (now also a soul) to make the adjustment. There is no enduring suffering, it is over instantly, and immediately, once he is in the Light, that soul is given a remembering of what that experience was for, why he agreed to it. But I cannot stress enough that under these kinds of circumstances, the soul does immediately leave the body and is not suffering. On this side, it's very difficult to grasp the idea of not being in the body. But pain belongs to the physical, and that soul is no longer physical, so there is no pain.

Does someone who has crossed due to an act of violence want her killer brought to justice?

Once she is there, justice is in the hands of God. It is not like here where we are so hell-bent on revenge, punishment, and retribution. Nobody "gets away with it" on the Other Side, but justice is not meted out in courts and prisons. It's karmic; God decides what is correct, and meanwhile, among souls, including someone whose physical life has been ended in such a way, there is only forgiveness. Hard to believe, maybe, but true.

What is your understanding about the soul of someone who has committed suicide?

This is a very difficult subject and I don't want to give an overly simple or wrong answer, but there is a lot about this that I don't understand. What I have been told, and virtually anyone knows this at a gut level to be true, is that there is nothing worse than taking a human life. That said, I do believe there is a difference between someone who willfully murders, and someone whose country sends him to war, and someone who accidentally kills another person, and someone who is in so much torment on this side that he ends his own life. What I believe is that on the Other Side there are different levels for these differences. Over there, it's not about judgment, it's about justice and forgiveness and healing. Spirit Masters will try to help the individual forgive and heal himself. It is the spirit—the one who killed himself— who must be able to forgive himself. This isn't easy because on the deepest possible soul level he knows he has done something wrong. Sometimes there will be a suicide where it's assumed that the person didn't really intend to take it that far, that it's a cry for help. In this case, an apparent attempt that unfortunately suc- ceeded might be deemed "accidental" by those who loved that person. A drug overdose and some kinds of single-vehicle ac- cidents might be called "accidental." But from what I understand, I do believe that even in those cases there was an element of in- tention; on some level the person really wanted to go, and so it's not entirely accidental. That soul will need to contend with her feelings about what she has done. She has lost the opportunity to fulfill that life's karma, and in so doing has created more karma for herself, created a situation where she will need to work to balance things in another lifetime. It's like in *On the Waterfront* when Marlon Brando throws the fight. Later he's sick about it. He says, "I coulda been a contender." If we throw the fight we reap regret. Those who commit suicide will have forgiveness from God, but they will have to struggle to forgive themselves.

Is there anything we can do on this side to help loved ones who have committed suicide find peace?

We can pray for them. They hear our prayers, and so does God, of course. It is so helpful for them to hear our positive thoughts and prayers for healing. We can say, "Please God, protect and keep them safe and let them find peace in their soul."

Who are our guardian angels, and do we meet them when we die?

We see all our loved ones and even will recognize others who we didn't even know here on this side, who have been with us before and who were helping us during our lives from the Other Side. These *are* our guardian angels.

Once we heal our lives, we're ready to start work again. Whereas before we *had* guardian angels, when we cross over we *become* guardian angels. We are given jobs—maybe we are sent to give guidance; we guide souls on this side to make good choices. Some of us, when we are there and understand all the ripple effect of things we've done, we have a hard time forgiving our behavior here. So some over there have the job of helping other souls over there, helping them to heal.

What is the difference between angels, spirits, souls, and guardians?

These are really false distinctions. A soul is a spirit, is an angel, is a guardian. They are all just different terms for the same thing. Even if an angel (or soul or spirit) isn't, right at that moment, pulling us out of the path of an oncoming car, it's still a guardian, still looking out for us.

What is a spirit guide?

Spirit guides have lived numerous lives on this side of the veil. Most will still be reincarnating again, although there are those who have evolved past the process of reincarnating—to put it the best way I can, they've gotten off what the Hindus refer to as the wheel of life. But for the most part, *teacher* and *spirit guide* are interchangeable terms.

Are there bad, or fallen, angels?

Yes, I do believe there are. Certainly everyone has heard of Lucifer. He was one of God's servants, I would say a Master spirit. I'm certain there are others too. There're plenty of horrible things that happen here. It seems like it would be an awful lot of work for one dark soul to accomplish. Even in my own life I've seen a number of individuals in whom I could sense evil at a gut level. I can't imagine it was the same soul, over and over, showing up in different bodies in the same lifetime. I don't think that's how it works.

What purpose would a fallen angel serve in this world?

I will never completely understand this piece of the puzzle. I think it'll be one of my first questions when I get over there, because they sure cause a lot of hurt over here. Maybe it's like the Garden of Eden—God just wanted to throw in some bad apples and say, "Okay, now what are you going to do with *that?*" I can only assume that facing evil challenges us to be our better selves, to not give in to it, to learn, to grow. When I get over there, God's gonna have some splainin' to do!

How do our guardian angels protect us?

Oh, I hear stories all the time about someone who came close to dying or being badly hurt who experienced what some might call "divine intervention." This is really our guardian angels, spirits from the Other Side who are looking out for us. One case that comes to mind is a young girl, Linda, who came to me and immediately her mother came through and had a lot to communicate, just a ton of stuff, and she said, "Mention the necklaces and say 'all my love.'" (This is something they very commonly ask me to say, "All my love." Usually they are showing me something of theirs that the person has that acts as a symbolic connection between the person who is still living and the person who has crossed.) So I tell Linda, "Your mother tells me to mention the necklaces and tell you 'all my love.' Do you have some necklaces of hers?" And Linda just collapses. She literally needed a wet washcloth to get herself revived and together. Then she tells me: When her mother died, she didn't have a lot of nice jewelry or anything—just costume jewelry and cheap, fun stuff. Linda wanted something to remember her mom, so she took three strings of beads—cheap, Mardi Gras–type necklaces. She wrapped them around and around the rearview mirror of her car, looping them many times so they wouldn't dangle down. One day, she's driving, and all of a sudden there's a truck headed right for her—there was nowhere for her to go, no way to get out of its way—it's going to be a head-on collision. She knows she's probably going to die, but as the truck bears down on her she just screams, "Mom!"

The next thing she knows, she's still alive. Her hand is in her lap and her fingers are wrapped around the three necklaces—which are all stretched out perfectly straight, lying across her lap!

Many times in my lifetime, the dead got me out of something. But with my own mortality, I know there may come a day when the spirits who are helping me might not be able to protect me. I know they will do the best they can, as far as they are allowed to intervene, but this is the place where we are in charge. We have to look out for ourselves and not totally rely on our deceased loved ones to always have our backs. We all just need to live each day fully and with joy and appreciation and hope for the best.

Besides protection, what other kinds of things do our guardian angels do for us?

One thing is that they give us counsel. Our conscience, for example, is made up of our own intelligence and our guardian angels. You've seen the cartoon of a good angel on one shoulder and a bad angel on the other. Where do you think the inspiration for that cartoon came from? Whoever was the first to draw that must have known—that's the way it literally is. When you think you are making a decision all on your own, you're really getting input from the souls of your loved ones who are looking out for you. Also, I do believe we are constantly being challenged by "negative energy." Like when there is a crying child and it just goes on and on and won't stop crying. The good angel says, "You're the adult, this is a child." It argues for you to understand your place, that you have the perspective of an older person and won't blame a child for crying. But the bad angel may say, "Smack it!" A lot of people will split the difference. They know they shouldn't hit the child, but they'll say something like, "If you don't stop crying I'll give you something to cry about." The negative energy is having an effect, but the inspiration and guidance of the good angel still keep them from giving in to it.

But there's really no limit to what our angels can help us with when we really need help. They won't just take care of our lives for us—we do have to make an effort, use our free will, make our own mistakes, learn our own lessons. But if you really really need a train to come, or a taxi on a dark night in lousy weather, or even a parking place, they can help out with that.

I get so much help from all those guys over there. One time I was going to this woman's house to do a group show, a "house party," and I was a little lost and felt anxious because I hate to be late. I saw a man in a uniform pointing and somehow knew he was directing me. When I got to the house I said, "I'm sorry I'm a little late. I was confused, but then I saw this man pointing me to the right place." I described the man and where he was standing. One of the guests—a woman—said, "Oh my goodness! That was my husband!" She told me her husband had been known affectionately as "the mayor of the street." He'd always tell people what to do with their garbage, when to cut their lawns. It happened that we were having our get-together on the day before the fifth anniversary of his death. The woman told me that he had always stood where I had seen him. His best friend lived there. He's crossed over, but he's still helping out in the neighborhood.

Another time I had an important business meeting and I asked Them to come to help me with an important conversation I was going to have. I said, "Please make me look good and be a star!" They said, "Sure, if you can get your big head through the door, we'll help."

Can the dead help us find things?

If you ask them to, they will help you. Otherwise, I think they like watching us go crazy, turning the house upside down when we misplace something. My husband, John, lost his keys once and he looked everywhere for them. John, being John, did not ask for help. After a month, he said to me again, "I can't find those keys anywhere." So I asked his father (who is deceased), "Leo, where are John's keys?" Here I should mention that we live in the middle of the woods on a very large property, and it was the dead of winter when my husband (finally, sort of) asked for help. By this time there was a layer of dead leaves and a fresh coat of snow over everything. Leo directed me to an exact spot on our property and told me to bend down and clear away the snow and the leaves, and there they were. As God is my witness, I did exactly that. I didn't have to try here and there; I didn't have to brush away a big area. I bent down one time, in one place, and the keys were right there. I called John at work to tell him that, with his father's help, I'd found his keys. I said, "Now do you believe me? Are you impressed?" And he responded in true John fashion, "Yes, I'm impressed. But I'll be even more impressed when you go out there with my father and ask him to show you where the million dollars is buried."

Do dead people watch us shower?
Does Grandma know I like to do *that* in bed?

Sure they do! And Grandma certainly does know. . . . They see us in the bathroom and they see us in the bedroom! But who cares? They're dead! Who're they gonna tell?

Don't freak out. The thing you need to remember is that they are not in the flesh—they *remember* the flesh, but it's not of any concern to them anymore. They're not judging. It's not like they're going, "Whoa! Has she got a big butt!" or "If I were him, I'da shaved that!" or "*Holy Moly!* Did ya ever see such a big . . . ?" Well, you get the point. The dead are not Peeping Toms—they don't get any special thrill out of watching, it's not entertainment to them—that's thinking in *human* terms. They just look at it like human nature, like we might see two animals going at it and just look at it as animal nature. We might smile, or even laugh. But it's not judgment. We don't expect a couple of dogs or squirrels to be embarrassed that we see them doing what they're doing. Yes, the dead certainly do see us in the shower or making love, but it's just like we might witness an ordinary act of human kindness. We don't judge it. We just smile and think, How beautiful. They are just happy that you are experiencing love or maybe just one-night-stand pleasure. They are happy for you. The dead are not nearly as stuffy about sex as some of us here can be—not even our dead *Sicilian* fathers!

And before you even ask the question—yes, they also see all our secret, sneaky behavior. They see us raiding the refrigerator and scarfing down the ice cream and the leftover lasagna when we're supposed to be on diets; they see us picking our noses when we can't find a Kleenex. Again, in their eyes, it's just ordinary human behavior. No judgment. They also see us in the operating room and in the classroom and at our holiday tables. They enjoy with us all the events we celebrate in our lives and they also walk us through our sorrows and heartaches.

Is it possible to ask the dead for a moment of privacy? Can we have a "Would you please avert your eyes, Grams?" moment with the Other Side?

I hate to break it to you, but, no. Even if you said, "Don't look," that wouldn't stop them. What about God? You never think about God looking, right? It's the same thing. Does God ever stop looking? No. When your grandparents are over there, they are one with God. You can't just turn that off or hide from it.

Do the dead have sex on the Other Side?

Boy, you've got a one-track mind!

No! They are energy forms so they don't have the same needs and desires of the flesh. They don't make love, they don't eat anything, and no, they don't go to the bathroom. They're in spirit form, not flesh. I know, you're probably thinking, "No food? No sex? I'm not going!"

Is there such a thing as a "dirty old ghost"?

Well, I didn't exactly say that the dead didn't have a sense of humor about the body and being in the flesh. They may touch someone or push someone, just to show that they can do it. I've twice had a spirit actually try to make love to me. Very strange, but not scary—of course, I can't speak for everyone on that count. But I've heard many stories about spirits touching someone. I had one client whose beach house down at the Jersey shore had a very playful resident ghost. He seemed to live in their shower and delighted in pressing up against anyone who used the shower—not every time, but often enough that the whole family was aware of it. When they had a guest at their beach house they'd get a kick out of it when the guest would use the shower. The person would come out of the bathroom with a weird look on her face and say something like, "You'll never believe this, but . . ." and they'd all go, "We know. Charlie!!!"

The dead are just having some fun with us. They like to joke about the body. We're in it, so we don't always get the joke or think it's funny. It's a struggle here on earth, being in physical form. We have good days and bad days. But I think you'll all agree with me when I say that when it's good, it can be pretty freakin' good!

Do the dead remember having sex?

They certainly do remember!

And that reminds me of a story: A couple of years ago, two women came to see me for a reading. They were old friends, either in their late seventies or early eighties, and had made their appointments together. They both wanted to hear from their husbands, and without any problem, both their husbands came through. Of course, they all knew one another and both husbands were joking around about their "date nights," which was really a euphemism for their night to have sex with their respective wives. So the one husband is talking about Wednesday night and the other is talking about Friday night. The one mentioned a restaurant. I asked his wife, who was there for the reading, "What about this restaurant?" Turns out that this couple used to go to the same place a few nights a week. Everybody knew them there, and they knew them so well that they knew about "Wednesday night." The waiter would always ask at the end of the meal, Do you want any dessert? But then he'd catch himself and say, almost winking, Oh, no, I know you wouldn't want dessert because I just remembered it's *Wednesday* and you'll want to get home! Her friend was laughing, until her own husband started talking about *Friday* nights and how she'd leave her hairnet on when they made love! So this got the first woman laughing, like, "At least I didn't wear a hairnet when I had sex!" It was so funny, like they were doing a comedy routine together with their dead husbands!

Do the dead miss their bodies?

I am under the impression that they don't miss their bodies, but they remember the flesh as enjoyable. They remember eating, they remember having sex. But they have a sense of humor remembering their earthly desires and pleasures. In all honesty, it's probably hard for most people to even relate to how it is there, because as spirit, we're not even male or female. We're completely asexual. We reincarnate as either gender because there are different lessons to be learned from each role and the spirit holds those memories. We're so identified with male or female, whatever we are, even if we'd identify ourselves as gay or bisexual. It's hard to get our heads around not having a body, not being either.

Another part of this is, during my readings, very often depressed or sad people will say that once they die they don't want to come back. I hear it all the time: "I want to stay on the Other Side" or "I hope this is my last time around." But once we're there, something makes us come back into the flesh so that we can learn lessons. I believe that everyone's ultimate goal is to become a spirit Master or spirit guide and to be a divine spirit who is close to God. To do this we have to be worthy. In the soul form, there is nothing more important than being worthy and being close to God. On this side, we want to be married and to have kids; we want money and beauty. In the energy form, nothing physical matters anymore; we care only about being close to God.

When we choose to come to this side, do we get to pick our bodies?

Partly yes and partly no. We will get the body that we need for whatever our mission is in this lifetime. All our attributes—our beauties and our flaws—will be selected both for us to learn lessons and also to enable us to succeed in our purpose. So it's such a combination of things that I don't think anyone could describe a formula. Each individual's case will be unique. For instance, if we are to be some kind of leader, we might get strong, attractive facial features, we'll be charismatic in some way, maybe we'll be tall. Not everyone who is a leader is tall and good-looking, of course, but it is likely that those who lack those qualities will have other items on their karmic agenda that they are working on this time so they've accepted the challenge of being a leader with fewer of the conventional attributes. Maybe someone like physicist Stephen Hawking is so focused in the life of the mind that the body is less important to him. I cannot imagine anyone choosing to be born with his degree of physical limitation, but he may have agreed to this lifetime's severe physical restraints knowing that he'd be able to accomplish his work, his mission, and also get to burn through some serious karma like rocket fuel—and then again he might not be able to imagine being born with what he might consider *my* limitations and restraints! Perhaps if we are here to learn humility, we may be born with certain flaws that would cause us to be humble. On the other hand, maybe you get extra points for looking like Audrey Hepburn and still being humble—I don't really know how these things go, I haven't seen the scoring system. Bottom line, I think, is that we might not get what we want, but we will get what we need.

What is it like on the Other Side? Is the Other Side actually a place?

Well, it isn't physical so to call it a "place" probably isn't accurate. It's more a "state" or a condition—it's *paradise*. It's like here except that it has a completely different quality to it. It's difficult to explain, but try to think of the worst thing anyone ever did to you your whole life. How bitter you are about that, how you might still, deep down, hate the person who hurt you so badly. On that side, that intense feeling of bitterness is completely gone. I have heard this over and over again from spirits. It's really unbelievable; it just doesn't exist. All is forgiveness, all is love.

The Other Side, of course, is not physical. But it does have many attributes that can *seem* physical. From what I have heard, anything we have here is also there, only more beautiful, pure, vibrant—somehow more real than what we know as reality even though our assumption would be that, when comparing physical versus spiritual, physical would be "more real." I've heard that there are plants and gardens just like here only the colors are more intense. Our pets run around free and we never have to worry about them being hit by a car. I've never seen one, but I've heard about grand cathedrals of crystal and light. I know that there are many levels and since we do retain our personalities we will naturally gravitate to one area or another and likely our experiences will be different.

The first time my father came to me after he crossed over, I asked him what he did on the Other Side. He told me that he and my brother Harold went for long rides in the mountains. This implies to me that he sees the mountains and he feels the mountains. There is no question in my mind that They have the ability to do that. I don't know how, because I am limited, but I do know that God is so grand and so great that it would not surprise me that God would give the souls that cross home the rewards they deserve.

Is there any color on the Other Side?

Yes, there is color and it is brilliant. They say we have true beauty on this side of creation, but this is nothing compared to what's on the Other Side. To understand why that might be, just remember, we have a hand in things on this side. God creates it and we destroy it. We pollute it. We litter it. We bulldoze forests or we ruin rich farmland and then we have climate changes and dust bowls and floods; we have the loss of entire species of creatures and all sorts of other consequences that destroy the original perfection. We do have heaven on earth here if we can just let it be that, but we don't. Just imagine if we could see the world "as is" from God, without people messing it up, and you might have some sense of the brilliance of the Other Side. I think this may have answered more than the question, but I feel better getting that off my chest.

Is it crowded on the Other Side?
Do we have to wait in lines?

No, there is never a space problem over there. It's paradise, it's perfection—plenty of parking for everyone. Everyone has a big apartment, no lines in the grocery store or waiting to get a lane at the bowling alley. How could it be paradise otherwise? Nobody has to leave to make room for anyone else—we all are pure energy. The Other Side is a dimension of pure energy. Space, in the terms we think of it, is virtually meaningless there.

Do the dead inhabit old houses?

That old myth is not really true—at least not in the way that it's usually portrayed in scary movies and books. I know that sometimes souls are connected to places they love, but I don't think it's like that in most cases. Most of the time, the dead will be around their loved ones, wherever they may be, not attached to a particular house.

Why is it that we hear about the dead haunting a particular place?

Sometimes a soul has a story to tell. For example, in historic places like a Civil War battlefield. Gettysburg is one of the most "haunted" places I've ever visited. There are just *so* many spirits there. In these cases, there is a story about an incomplete life being cut down. Our history books tell only the smallest part of the story. We will never understand the real experience. And sometimes the dead do linger in these places in order to tell their stories. In a way the souls here are "stuck." They might not understand that it was their karma to die at that point, and might feel they've been prevented from completing their purpose. Think about it—when we're stopped from doing something we want very badly to do, we get really frustrated. Maybe we feel it wasn't our fault and we get caught up in making excuses, telling our story, so others will know it wasn't our fault. In the case of these souls, if they would cross, on the Other Side everything would be explained and they'd be encouraged to accept God's love. But if they don't cross and get their life review, and perspective, they don't have a clue. They literally are lost souls. This really doesn't happen a lot. If it happened every time someone was murdered there would be a thick painful energy all around us. But where the story is important, some souls move on and some stay. In any case, they forgive the minute they go into the Light. In the Light there is no room for anything but forgiveness and love.

Are there souls who are "stuck" in limbo? How can a soul get out of limbo?

As I understand it, limbo is a state of frustration due to not understanding. A soul does not understand what is expected of it, what it has done wrong, and cannot go forward; it can't get to the next level in its spiritual development.

To escape limbo the soul must be willing to listen to and heed the spirit Master or guide—like a guidance counselor. For example, maybe a kid thought it would be a good joke to get all the students out of class by setting off the fire alarm. He's reported and he's expelled from school. But he just thought it would be funny, no big deal, he doesn't understand why he's in trouble. So the guidance counselor maybe gives him an example of why his actions weren't quite right. Then the kid gets it. He has understanding, realizes what he did was wrong, even if he didn't intend anything bad by it. He can apologize and get back into his classes. If he doesn't get the understanding, and he's let back into class, he may do the same thing again or something worse. But with the understanding he's able to move on. In spiritual terms, it's the same thing. We can't get to the next level without gaining the understanding of the level we're on. Once we do, we're given a new chance, a new mission that we can set off on with an improved attitude.

Is it hard for you to visit historic sites?

In spite of the fact that it's always a very emotional experience for me, I do enjoy visiting these kinds of places and hearing the stories there. At the Alamo, even just walking in the dirt around the fort was a very moving experience. You can feel the horses, the men, smell and taste the very blood. I don't think you need to be psychic to experience this—it's so strong. When I visited the Anne Frank House in Amsterdam the souls surrounding that place were completely overwhelming to me. Actually, I could feel the souls throughout the old part of the city. Amsterdam is breathtakingly beautiful. Walking in the streets, along the canal, in the very stones of the buildings, they all hold the vibrations of the history that has taken place there, you can feel the energy. Apart from the beauty, I, and others, I'm sure, can't escape the energy of all the souls still lingering there. Both the innocent and the evil. Those who were killed and those who killed. When I do a reading, I am emotionally removed and uninvolved. But this is a very different experience for me. I do get very emotional. At the Anne Frank House, I was just crying and crying. A woman said to me, "Are you all right? Did you lose your family?" This is the downside of being a medium, I guess, this extreme sensitivity to others and what happens to them. I just have such extreme empathy. But this is not something that just I can feel. So many feel drawn to places like this. Our souls are drawn to connect with these stories.

And if you're wondering whether I heard from Anne Frank while at the house, the answer is no, she's not there. The spirit who was Anne Frank is a Master and would not be held in limbo in that way, attached to a place. She had a mission and a purpose in that lifetime and she accomplished that. Her life was brief, but what she accomplished was so powerful that it continues to resonate to this day. She has moved on.

Do all places in which humans have lived hold vibrations?

Anything we have touched will retain some energy. Old things and old places naturally have more, and by "old places" I mean places where people have been for a long time, or where events with a lot of intensity have taken place, where a lot of human emotion was spent, so to speak. Joy, awe, sadness, horror. You can tell the difference between the energy in an old home and the energy in a brand-new, just built suburban development home. The new home has no emotional patina, far less energy than a place that has been around for years and has had "history" made within it. Also, old objects, especially ones that have been handled a lot, will have this energy. Clothes that have been worn will have this. Judy Garland's ruby slippers are in the Smithsonian Institution now, but just imagine if you could get them out of that glass case and touch them. What if you could step into them! If I were a size five, that would be totally awesome!

Can the dead talk with one another?

Yes, definitely. Not talk, exactly, language is irrelevant. They communicate by thought, telepathically. Thought is universal. If you are thinking "I'm hungry," that thought is the same no matter what language you speak. Over there, spirits talk in heavenly IM.

Does everybody know everybody else there? Do we communicate with spirits we never knew on earth?

Oh yes. Bear in mind that on the Other Side we may have grandparents or other ancestors we never even met on earth, who crossed before we were born, so we knew them only in spirit, and now we are meeting them in spirit again. There are also souls with whom we have no family or friend connection, but even these we will "know" instinctually and would relate to and communicate with as another human being (albeit in spirit form). The best way I can explain this is, think about if aliens came and colonized the earth. We'd recognize and relate to other humans, as opposed to the aliens, as fellow earthlings. We may not know them personally, but we think of them as "like us," and if we wanted to ask directions from someone it's more likely we'd ask another earthling than an alien. We'd just feel more comfortable. Over there, everyone is "like us."

Do the dead still retain their five senses?

No. Our five senses are "of the body," and of course the dead are "of the spirit." They can't smell or taste anything, but they don't eat anything anymore so it's really not like a loss; it's no big deal. They can't feel anything themselves, but they can touch us. It's not a physical touch, like with a finger. It's energy, so it feels like a small electric shock—not strong enough to hurt anyone, but enough to startle you.

How do the dead get around?

It's pretty much instantaneous in terms of travel time. It's as quick as thought. In fact, it is thought. They simply change their thoughts to another place or person, and there they are—right where they want to be. The psychic autobahn!

Are the dead always with us—even on vacation?

Absolutely—just like the air is always with us. If you are taking a bus, they are going. If you're flying, they're going—first class without paying extra for their ticket.

At one of my big shows there was a woman who was looking for her father. He came through right away and I asked her, "Are you going on vacation?" And she didn't really know what I was talking about and then I said, "Are you going to Hawaii? Because your father says he's really excited about going with you to Hawaii." What really happened was he was showing me an image of a lei and that symbolized Hawaii to me, so I said, "Are you going to Hawaii?" In a way when I do readings I'm always putting the pieces of a puzzle together so they will make sense for the person I'm talking with. But it's an art not a science—like if I see palm trees and a beach, I think of Florida. But it might be the Bahamas—I don't really know. Or if I hear a snippet of the song "Blue Hawaii," maybe it has something to do with the person going to Hawaii. But it also could be that they just like Elvis! So when I asked this woman if she was going to Hawaii, she said that her son lived in Hawaii and they went there fairly often, and yes, she was going to Hawaii soon, but it wasn't really a vacation, which is why she didn't know what I was talking about at first. That was just my assumption, in trying to piece the puzzle together. My point is, whether for a vacation or just a regular visit, her father was going, just the same!

Meanwhile, as I told her that her father was excited about going on the trip I saw the pained and shocked look on her husband's face—it was like "Oh, great! Your *dad* is coming with us?" He was probably thinking, "Does that mean your dad can watch what we're up to behind closed doors? *Real* romantic." But since I've already answered that question, what he might also have been thinking was, "Why can't he go visit your sister in Baltimore and give us a little alone time?" The thing is that—if she *had* a sister in Baltimore—her father wouldn't have to choose between them, he could be with both. God is in all places at all times. When we are here, we're *part* of God, but when we go back, we are *one* with God. We're energy. Hawaii, Baltimore, New Jersey, or the North Pole—we're everywhere at once.

Can the dead travel back in time?

I have met souls who are from the 1800s, for example, but it's not that they are traveling back in time. That's just the last time they were here. If you are in the Light of God, if paradise to you is being in a Roman city, you have the ability there to be in Rome and do as the Romans do. You can go to another century if that is what you prefer.

Can they travel to the future?

I know that they know things that will happen in the future, that have to do with our destiny, and also they have told me some things about how our technology will develop. But can they actually go to the future? They don't travel ahead; they have information that is all-knowing involving the future.

What do the dead wear?

Nothing. It's like trying to put clothes on the invisible man. You can't do it. Sometimes they will appear to me in clothing, just so they will be recognizable to the person receiving a reading—for instance, it's very common for someone to show me a uniform of some kind, whether it's for a particular job or the military, or maybe I *hear* (but don't actually see) that this person was a real snappy dresser. But for the most part they are commando. They are an energy form. They are like a shadow. And shadows don't like to be burdened by Prada or Louis Vuitton purses. Anyone can tell that *I'm* not dead yet. I have never met an accessory I did not like! Bring on the bling! Gimme the bangles, baubles, and beads—and while you're at it, the Chanel sunglasses! Then help me hide the credit card bills from my husband.

Do the dead ever try to give you fashion advice?

No, they leave that to John! As much as I love dressing up and wearing big jewelry, John is the real clotheshorse and fashion police in our family. He's very particular about his appearance and if we go to the mall I better not even ask him to carry a bag from Sears!

I remember right after I first went public, I was asked to do a private Halloween party and John offered to drive me. I thought it would be nice to have him along because I was a little unsure of myself and thought he'd be good moral support. But as soon as I got in the car, John looked over at me, eyeing my sweater. It was black, decorated with a big orange pumpkin on the front. (I also had on these really cute, dangly ghost earrings for the occasion.) He says, "Is that what you're wearing?" and I knew by his tone that it was not what he would recommend. He clearly thought a pumpkin sweater was not appropriate attire for a hired psychic. I got a little huffy; I said, "Well what would you suggest, John? Do you think I should maybe be wearing a turban? Maybe a bunch of beads or a medallion? Did I forget my crystal ball?" He knew to let it drop.

When we arrived at the party I discovered that I was not the only psychic for the event. Two of us had been hired, and when I saw the other one I almost burst out laughing. That one would have had John's seal of approval. Full regalia: turban, medallion, crystal ball.

Do the dead appear in color?

Not to me. No color, no size, no shape. Only on rare occasions when they are trying to give me a clue as to their identity that I can pass along to someone I'm doing a reading for. But even then, it's more a mist or haze.

Do the dead have emotions?

They can tell what we might be feeling at the moment. They feel total joy and complete forgiveness. There is no room for anger, sadness, or fear on the Other Side. I can only relate it to when something so amazing happens and you are overcome with so much happiness that you forget everything that had been bothering you. You are simply beyond any type of negativity. Your mother-in-law cannot faze you. Your boss cannot make you mad. You are too happy for that. That level of happiness and joy is what They are constantly experiencing. They don't sit around thinking, "Oh, she is *so annoying*," or, "Geez, I can't *stand* him." They don't have time for all of that. Annoyances and angers are not acknowledged. They choose joy and love and forgiveness— even when it comes to mother-in-laws (or so I am told).

Do we still experience depression when we are dead?

Not as such. But I do think that even on that side there can be an experience of sorrow in the soul—at least when we first get there—which can come from realizing that we had a chance and screwed it up. Other souls will try to help a given soul get over that. Someone who was an alcoholic on this side and maybe ruined his own life and made other people miserable will realize his past mistakes when he crosses over and may be extremely upset about how he lived his life. He'll see all of his errors and all the pain he caused and it will take him a while to get over this.

At one of my big shows I did a reading for a woman who wanted to know whether her ex-husband had even made it to the Other Side. Clearly she thought he might have been relegated to some "other" place. He did come through—she was pretty surprised when I told her that, in fact, he actually was there—and he was apologizing like crazy, saying that she had been right. I didn't know what he was talking about (although she said that she did); I had the sense that maybe he took bad advice from someone he trusted, it seemed like a family thing. But the understanding I got was that he had treated her very badly, really put her through hell. Over there, he realized the error of what he had done and wanted her to know how sorry he was.

Are our pets waiting for us on the Other Side?

Of course they are. Animals are gifts from God. They give us comfort and joy, they sustain us. In all honesty, our pets give us the nearest thing to unconditional love we can know on this side. We need to treat them with respect, and never take them for granted. Just like the people who have passed on who are near to us, you can hear from them. Often when I'm doing a reading someone on the Other Side will tell me to tell my client, "Your dog is here."

Sometimes a pet doesn't even wait for you to cross, they come back and visit you on this side. I've heard numerous stories of pets who have been seen in ghost form, or heard barking, or even felt. My friend Ginger and her partner Wendy were sleeping one night and Ginger was wakened by this feeling of her dog Nino Guiseppe jumping all over her and licking her face, just like he used to do when he was a puppy. She knew realistically it couldn't be, so the next morning she said to Wendy, "I had this dream last night that Nino was in the bed and jumping all over me and licking my face," and Wendy said, "I don't think that was a dream, because I felt him too!"

Are pets the only animals on the Other Side, or do all animal souls go there too?

I don't have all the answers. I'm not sure how all this works. But any living creation is the energy of God, that God created and that goes back to God. How it goes back and where I'm not sure. If you have a wild turkey or a fox and it dies, it goes back to the Light, to the universe that is God. I'm not sure in what form. Does it go back as a fox? I'm not sure, but I do know that it goes back.

Are there spirits from other planets among the dead on the Other Side?

I really don't know. The universe is a big place, so it wouldn't be a huge surprise if there were, but I wouldn't know. I know only about those I have access to, and I have access only to those with a connection to the person I'm doing a reading for. I touch the person, ask permission to listen, and ask them who they are looking for. As far as I know, I've never done a reading for an alien so I've never been in contact with an alien spirit over there. But you never know who might make an appointment next—let me get back to you on that one.

On the Other Side, can we communicate with animals, too, as we do with people here?

Even on this side we can have a deep connection and communication with animals, especially our pets. Our pets are also our protectors, just like our guardian angels. My friend Craig told me about his Jack Russell terrier, Earl, who saved his life. Craig was working out in his yard and he didn't see that there was a poisonous snake in front of him. In complete oblivion, Craig was headed right toward the snake. Earl launched himself between Craig and the snake and the snake bit him. Fortunately, Earl didn't die, but that dog was completely selfless—if either he or Craig was going to be bitten, he wanted to make sure it was him.

On the Other Side I believe our ability to communicate with animals is enhanced, but I think it is in a very simple form. It would be telepathic, as we communicate with other human souls, but maybe the ideas we expressed would have to be more simple, not sophisticated. For instance, I don't think you'd suddenly be having a philosophical discourse with your Irish Setter, but maybe with your Siamese.

Is it true that cats are psychic and can see the dead? If so, are they the only animals that can do this, or do all animals see ghosts?

Cats aren't the only ones. All animals have a sixth sense. One of my friends lost her boyfriend and her dog kept seeing him. She'd hear her dog barking and go into the bedroom and the smell of cigar smoke would be really strong. Her boyfriend always used to smoke cigars so she knew it was him, but her dog would always be the one to alert her first.

Do the dead go to ball games?

Yes, sure. But their way of being a spectator is different from ours. They may watch a loved one playing baseball. Or they may watch a loved one watching a game. But they are watching because we belong to them. I don't think they're watching to see who wins or loses— they're not betting on the Subway Series!

Even if the dead don't bet on ball games, weren't there a lot of happy Red Sox fans in heaven in 2004?

Truthfully, I don't really think, from what I know about the Other Side, that anyone was really waving foam fingers around. I think they knew why the Sox won that year, and why they hadn't won in other years. But what I can say is that anyone over there, who had a Sox-loving loved one still here, would have been happy for their loved one, even if they also appreciated that in the scheme of things winning a ball game or even a series is not that big a deal. They do appreciate it when we are happy.

Do the dead go to bars?

There are many dimensions of God, but I don't really think that a bar scene is one of them—even though there may be plenty of spirits in a bar. The dead don't drink so I'm thinking that there are not bar crawls on the Other Side. A Sex on the Beach or a Fuzzy Navel would no longer hold any meaning for them.

Do the dead listen to music?

Well, there is a Hall of Records on the Other Side, but it's not what it sounds like. It's not some big CD collection. And the angels are not jamming or hip-hopping up there. But there is definitely music. In fact, the Other Side is the source of music, they channel it to us, to those on this side who we think of as composers—they really are just receiving a channel. I am honestly not sure how it works. Obviously, it comes from God, it doesn't originate with a particular soul on the Other Side as opposed to a soul on this side. But I don't know what the mechanism is. What I can tell you is that, believe it or not, all music is intended for healing. What can I say? You may hate opera, or rap, or reggae. You may grimace at jazz, or tango music, or rock and roll. Classical music may leave you utterly cold or disco might make you gag. But all souls vibrate with a different frequency; we're not all tuned to the same station, and with music it truly is a case of different strokes for different folks. What makes one person insane will be music to the ears and healing to the spirit of another. Music has the power to both calm and invigorate us and we don't need to translate it to any other language—it can be appreciated universally. It's magical medicine and all of it comes from over there. Mozart was a child when he began composing, Beethoven was deaf and still wrote music that has lasted through the ages. Their compositions were channeled to them, from God, as all other music has been channeled through all other musicians in this world.

Do the dead keep a schedule?

No. The word does not even *exist* on the Other Side. Often when I'm doing a reading and I get a prediction from someone over there, my client will ask, "When is that going to happen?" Well, sometimes they will give me a number—let's say they tell or show me the number 2. I don't know if that means two hours, two days, two weeks, two months, two years. I might be able to get a little more info and tell the client that it *seems* like they mean two weeks. But this is a very imperfect method.

Sometimes they will mention a birthday, but it won't be clear whether it's a birthday that has just passed, or is just coming up. It can be a bit of a guessing game where the client has to give confirmation—I have no clue!

The dead have jobs, but don't have to punch a clock. They don't have appointments, but very often they will be aware of a big event coming up for a family member—maybe a graduation or a wedding, or some other family gathering, and they'll tell me to tell my client, "I'll be there!"

Do the dead obey rules?

Yes, we all do. But honey, they also break them! But seriously, I'm sure there are a few rules God has made, but I'm also sure they are simple ones.

Do we know when it is our time to die?

Yes, we all know that, in the core of our soul. Most of the time, though, we don't have access to what we know, or we don't know it consciously, but still we'll behave in a way that in retrospect we might say, "Boy, he was always in a hurry. He must have known." We have three levels of awareness. At the first level we're aware of the input we are getting from our five physical senses. At the next level we have our introspection and our memories. Then there is our supraconsciousness, which is our "knowing" of our connection to God and all that entails. It's at this third level where we do know how long our time on earth will be. Like I said, usually we are not focused on that level, but sometimes, in some people, it bleeds through.

One time, two sisters came to see me and told me the story of their brother, who was always saying, at different times, when he was talking about things he might like to do in his life, "Well, if I make it to thirty . . ." It really bothered his sisters; they hated that he would suggest that he might not live till the age of thirty. They always said to him, "Don't say that!"

When he was twenty-eight, he met and fell in love with a girl and they got engaged. They decided to get married in Antigua and they chose his thirtieth birthday for their wedding date. After the wedding, he and his new wife were swimming and all of a sudden it got very dark and a storm came up. They swam for the shore, but the water was all choppy with a strong current. He turned to his wife and said, "I'm not going to make it." She said, "Of course you're going to make it! Come on!" But he drowned.

He had everything to live for. He wasn't unhappy. He didn't commit suicide. He just *knew* this was his day.

On the other hand, at one of my big shows in Verona, New Jersey, there was an elderly woman who was looking for her husband, Mike. Her daughters were with her in the audience. Mike did come through and to identify himself to his family he told me all about his projects, most of them unfinished, and all the stuff he collected in his backyard to build things with "someday." He showed me this image of his yard—all sectioned off and filled with junk, concrete blocks, you name it. He had a real sense of humor about it, was actually making fun of himself, and his daughters were smiling and nodding, like, "Yep. That's our dad." But then Mike has something serious to communicate. He tells the woman, his wife, that she has to stop asking him to come and get her; Mike says it's not her time, she has to stay here, that there is something more for her to do for the family. She is nodding her head, reluctantly, I can tell, and tears are streaming down her face. Mike tells me to assure her that when it *is* her time, he promises to come get her, and he promises she won't suffer. She was more than ready to go, but it wasn't her time. Even though she *wanted* to go, she did seem to know and understand that.

Do the dead feel bad if we never visit them at the cemetery?

No, because they are not there. The cemetery is purely for the living so that we have a place to associate with our loved ones. They do hear our thoughts there, but they hear our thoughts no matter where we are—the funny thing is that they are just as likely to be in the car with us as we are driving *to* the cemetery—it really isn't necessary to sit next to a gravestone to talk to a spirit who has crossed. Really, leaving flowers and gifts at the gravesite is meant to provide comfort to the grieving friends and family members. For us, things we place on a grave are symbols of our love. But most likely They would be saying to us, "Don't waste your money on those flowers, hon."

Do souls who have crossed miss us as much as we miss them?

I don't think so, because they're here with us. Look at it this way: Right now, if you had relatives who lived in another state—let's say you lived in New Jersey and they lived in Florida—you can't see them all the time. Maybe you miss them, but you aren't grieving that you don't see them. Now let's say you could lift out of your body and, just by thinking of it, be poolside or hanging out with them in some nice air-conditioned mall. They can't see or hear you, but you see and hear them. As a rule, this ability to be close to loved ones still living seems to be pretty satisfying to those who have crossed over. I think the only time They might feel anything like grief of this kind is if there was some unfinished business, or something they had wanted to say. But even then they are in a place of total peace and forgiveness so I don't think it's the same.

Do the souls of our loved ones ever want to come back to us? Are they sorry they left?

I have never had a soul tell me they are sorry they left. Maybe they are not entirely happy about the circumstances of their crossing, but that's something different—they don't want those they've left on this side to be upset and grieving their loss so deeply. If they have left someone suffering or left someone feeling guilty, they are sorry for this.

Remember, we are not of this physical world. Ultimately we belong to the larger universe that is God. We're here in this small part of the universe to study and learn and have certain experiences that only the physical world can offer. Dying and being on the Other Side is like summer vacation. It's a rare child who will say that she wishes she could go back to school before September, and likewise I've never heard a soul express the wish to go back before it's her time to reincarnate. Once they are on the Other Side, they understand the journey they've just completed. They love us still. Their love lasts through eternity. But the Other Side is paradise and unlimited and they don't need to come back into physical form to be with us.

Can you explain how you communicate with the spirits of people who have passed away? What is the physical process?

The best way I can describe this is that I'm going on automatic pilot. Have you ever emptied the dishwasher or ironed a shirt? Probably a million times. So you don't think about it. You don't have to focus on anything, you don't really have to bring your mind to it. It's the same thing when I want to do a reading. I just stop thinking about it. The body goes into a lower heart rate, an alpha state. I don't hear a voice, it's a thought. And I might also see a flash of images. The family or other loved ones of the person having a reading (my client) shows up as a group to communicate. Around the client is energy—it's an out-of-focus arc or horseshoe around the person. This is a gathering of the various souls' energies. Sometimes I might also see a "pillar" of energy, which may be a tall person or a grandfather. When the reading begins, the energy around the client is hazy. Then, as the reading progresses, the energy is used up and it gradually clears or gets more focused.

If I'm doing a show with a lot of people, sometimes during a particular reading I will hum a few notes. This isn't any special song, I'm not calling up my spirit guides or anything; it's random. All I am doing is trying to block out sound around me. This puts me back in a subconscious state.

Every now and then I take a very strong short intake of breath. A lot of people ask me about this because it sounds strange and obviously they think it has something to do with my being able to let a message come through. Actually, all I'm doing is breathing! When I'm listening so intently to what they are saying to me, it's like I'm thinking, talking, and breathing almost through the top of my head. Of course, you can't breathe through the top of your head, so what's actually happening is that I'm *not* breathing. All of a sudden I realize I need air and I take a breath that is almost a gasp because I'm just grabbing it so fast.

Another thing I do is I hold my fingers pinched together. I don't really know why, but this somehow helps me to hold energy in, to conserve it in some way. Often you'll see pictures of spiritual Masters or even just an ordinary person meditating and they are holding their fingers like this. It must be something that I just picked up instinctively, because it's not anything I was told.

All mediums experience the dead differently. They won't be drastically different in the larger experience or the messages. However, some mostly see the dead—those are called *clairvoyants*. Some mostly hear the dead—they are *clairaudient*. Some get an overall impression—they're called *clairsentient*. The dead are energy and there's a lot of room there for different experiences and interpretation.

Do mediums receive messages through tarot cards?

A true medium who uses tarot cards is not really getting a message from the cards themselves. When I first went public I used the cards just to have something to focus on because I was nervous and, to be honest, I probably looked like I was going to have a seizure. I put the cards between me and the client and told the client I was using them to tap into the energy of their loved one. But really I was listening, not even looking, and sometimes I'd be staring up into space and talking with the cards all spread out in front of me and the client would say, "Whadderya looking up *there* for?" After a while I realized it was better just to sit there and talk with them without the set dressing.

Have you ever used a Ouija board?

I never want to be associated with Ouija boards. That is a dangerous game. You are opening a window and unless you know how to protect yourself you can call an evil soul who can haunt you and interfere with your life. When I do a reading, I always ask that God protect me and my home, and to let only those who walk in the Light come to me. I'm like Joan Crawford with her wire hangers: *No—Ouija—boards! EVER!*

How do you actually get the messages you receive during a reading?

They come in bits and pieces. Really, it's like putting together a jigsaw puzzle. I try to gather up the pieces and then the client has to put the picture together. Of course, if I think I know where a piece goes, I tell them.

First I try to identify the person on the Other Side who's talking—one person—stick with him, and let him introduce me to others. It's kind of like walking into a party and starting to talk with someone, and then he gradually brings you into the mix. I'll ask the spokesperson (mentally, usually not aloud), "Please step forward, do you have a message? Can you help me?" He does the heavy lifting.

In identifying himself, he might tell me his name outright. Or I might get just a first letter. When it's the latter, I tell the client, but I might also suggest possible names that go with that letter—just to jog the client's mind I might say, "It's a *J*—is it Jerry? John? Jack?—because I find so often that the client is in a state of mild shock to have this connection, even if they have come to me expressly to have it. Names are something that I'm less than perfect on—and for that I can only apologize. The spirit on the Other Side will tell me the name and I do try and frequently will get it dead on. But I'm not God. If I tell someone, it's a *D*—David, Donald, Dominick . . . I hope they won't be surprised if it's Donahue—but usually I can give enough other details about the person so that there is no doubt in the client's mind. Often to verify who is speaking I'll ask how they crossed over and they'll show me how they died. I might see that they were horizontal and often this means that they were in bed—whether they had a lingering illness or died in their sleep. Or I might feel a sensation in my chest and ask the client, "Did she have something the matter with her lungs?" I get all different sorts of feelings, like I'm being hit, or a sensation of having water in my lungs, or like having the wind knocked out of me, depending on what they are trying to tell me. It's never the same. Or I might see something going through the whole body and ask the client, "Was it cancer?" Or I might actually see blood and know that it was an accident or something worse. But I do this only so the client can know that the person I'm talking with is who they want to be in touch with. Sometimes they will actually name a specific illness, like diabetes, for instance. Sometimes dead people don't want to tell me how they died—it's still upsetting to them (often this is in the case of an overdose or some other thing that they are "ashamed" of or haven't yet healed from) or they don't want to upset the person here by talking about it.

I hear them much more than I see them. They speak to me in soft whispers. I do get images, though, if there's something specific they want me to describe. Or I might smell smoke—cigar, cigarette, or pipe smoke—or alcohol or a particular cologne that will be recognizable to the person I'm doing the reading for. I can say, "Was your uncle Louie a smoker? Because I can smell it on him." Sometimes I'll hear a melody, which is a bit of a problem for me because I'm not much of a singer, but if I recognize it, I do my best to convey it to the client and often he'll know what it means.

It can be that they come for only a few fleeting seconds, which happens quite often. The dead are an energy source and they have only a certain amount of energy, so they rarely stay too long. As soon as they come to me, they try to give me the most important messages that they want me to pass along, and most of the time they leave pretty quickly after that. If they come to me collectively, with several friends and family members, the meeting will last longer since they feed off one another's energy.

How long does the typical reading last?

This is something that many people find surprising because they are used to the notion of going to a card reader and having what is really a consultation. A reader will lay out the cards in a particular spread and go over them one by one, which can take quite a while and the client might be asking questions along the way. It's not unusual for this kind of reading to last half an hour or an hour. What I do is shorter but much more intense. The client is in direct contact with a spirit he recognizes and can validate, and a lot of information will be given in maybe just ten minutes. Then the spirit is gone. If multiple spirits show up, it can go to fifteen minutes, but longer than that would be very unusual.

When a medium is requested to speak with a particular spirit, does that spirit get pulled away from whatever it was doing on the Other Side to come through?

No, of course not. Nobody is pulling them away any more than God is being pulled away to hear our prayers when He's already listening to somebody's prayer in Italy. They are not limited so it's no problem for them to be everywhere at once. They are always available to us.

Do you have any control over who comes through when you do a reading?

I have control over keeping a negative energy out. I always start out saying that only those in the Light of God may speak to me. I won't have any negative entity around me. Not in my presence or in my home. I want no association with anything that does not come from God.

Can you zoom in somehow on a particular spirit? Can you choose who comes through?

Well, first I will ask my client's permission to listen. I will touch her hand and ask her to say her name and that will in some way alert the Other Side that we will be looking for someone with a connection to this person, my client. Then the person who is getting the reading has control over who comes to speak with her. She can ask for a particular person. Or if there are several people there that I describe, the person can say, "I just want to talk to my father," and the others will go away. There are some cases where spirits on the Other Side have an apology they want to give or may have a message that they want to have sent to someone. They don't get that many chances to connect with people here on this side and don't want to miss the opportunity, so they will be insistent.

Is it really necessary to ask your clients for their permission to listen?

I just think it's polite. If I don't get permission I feel that it's like eavesdropping. I mean, if I come visit you, I'm going to ring your doorbell, right? I'm not going to pull back your drapes and leave my nose print on the glass to see if you're home. It's only courteous to ask first. I try to give the respect that I'd like to get.

Do you ever hear from people that your client doesn't know?

Oh, very often! Nobody can know all the family members who have crossed before them. Frequently there is a spirit whom the living person has not even met in this lifetime, but who has a special relationship with that person as a soul over a number of lifetimes and he is checking in. Or sometimes it is a member of the extended family or even the deceased relative of a neighbor, someone with a connection of some kind to the family on this side. I've had people come for readings who will tell me, "You know, you were doing a reading for my neighbor and my family was mentioned." The spirit is just using my client as a messenger. I always tell my married clients that if a name is mentioned and they don't recognize it, it could be someone in their spouse's family since everyone is together over there and his family and hers are all seen as one.

I once was doing a reading for a new client and her mother-in-law came through. I had no idea that her husband's mother had crossed when her husband was still in college and she and her husband had not met or married until twenty years later so I didn't know that she had never met her mother-in-law. Anyway, the mother-in-law gave my client some messages for her husband, and then she was showing me a kitchen cupboard and some little thing of hers that she said my client had saved in her cupboard, and she said that it made her happy that my client had kept it and would occasionally take this object out and look at it and think of her. I knew for sure that it wasn't dishes—it was some small tchotchke kept in her kitchen cupboards—but my client said she didn't have any idea what her husband's mother was talking about; she said she'd ask her husband when she got home. But then something clicked for me and I asked my client whether her husband had a sister. She said, Yes, she did. I told her, "I got that wrong, it's his sister who has the little thing in her kitchen cupboard—you need to tell your sister-in-law what her mother said." As soon as her reading was over, my client called her sister-in-law and told her about the reading and asked whether she knew what her mother had been talking about. She said, "Oh my God, I have my mother's charm bracelet in a little cup in my kitchen cupboard and I do take it out and look at it and think of her very often."

When they want to get a message through, they will use any opportunity they get. Even on this side, you know, if you really want something you will be resourceful about getting it. They are like that, too. If they see the phone line open, they will grab the chance to talk.

Is it "safe" to be read in a group setting? Would a spirit ever reveal something that I might not want others to know?

If your concern is being embarrassed, then let me tell you it makes no difference, private or group, the dead would never intentionally humiliate anyone. They might say how proud they are of you for something and that might embarrass you if you embarrass easily, but the message is never anything ugly. Furthermore, they rely on me to deliver their messages appropriately, and *I* would never say anything ugly. As I've already said, I curse like a truck driver and have a pocketbook full of dirty jokes— which I thoroughly enjoy. But I don't get any kick whatsoever out of making someone feel bad. That just isn't going to happen. Over there it's all love. You need to remember that: *They love you.* The last thing they want is to do anything to hurt you, even if your relationship was hurtful while they were on this side. What I have seen happen is that a spirit might want to communicate an apology for something he did or the way he treated someone. That can be emotional, but I certainly hope not humiliating to the person receiving the message. They don't tell me what their apology is for, and even if I had a guess about it, I wouldn't say. The most I would say—the most I usually even know—is maybe that it was something pretty bad, or at least something that the spirit feels very bad about. If a client wants to elaborate on any message, that is up to her. On occasion a client might say something like, "He abused me from the time I was six until I left home at sixteen." That's something that person felt she needed to get out and felt she was in a place where she felt safe saying it. I have a big Kleenex box in my office. Often when I'm doing a reading for someone it's very emotional. A lot of people cry and even though I try to stay emotionally removed so I can be an effective messenger, sometimes *I* cry. Sometimes people seem embarrassed that they get emotional, but I always say, "That's what connects you, me, and the rest of the world! If I have to replace that box every two weeks, so be it!" I'm proud of it!

Was there ever a time when someone came for a reading and you didn't hear anything?

Yes, this has happened. In all the thousands and thousands of readings I've done, this has happened to me a couple of times. One time, three women in their early thirties had come to see me. The first two had readings and they had gone completely normally. Then with the third young woman, I just could not hear or see anything. I was a little freaked out since it had never happened before, but all I could do was say, "I'm sorry, honey. I can't take your money, I can't tell you anything." She was upset and left the house quickly. Her two friends hung back a bit and I said, "I don't know what happened, is there anything you can think of, any reason why there wouldn't be anything there?" And her friends said that she had a tendency to sabotage all her relationships and that what had happened with me had happened to her before a few times. She'd been to see other psychics, some the boardwalk variety, but also she had gone to see the famous psychic George Anderson, and he hadn't seen anything either!

Another time this happened, again it was a young woman in her early thirties, and when I told her that I was sorry, that I didn't see or hear anything, she seemed to take it very much in stride. She said, "That's okay. I'd rather you be honest with me."

To this day, I'm not sure why this happens. I can only guess it must be something karmic with those individuals. Without mentioning names, I do know that this has happened to other legitimate mediums, some famous and others who are real, but not famous. I have to assume that, although rare, this is a real phenomenon. The difference between a legitimate medium and a boardwalk psychic is, in a case like this, the legitimate medium will tell you that she can't hear anything. The fake is likely to make something up that she thinks you want to hear.

When you are reading for a large group are you ever confused about who is talking to whom?

Yes, this does happen. I call it "bleeding over"—when messages for someone nearby come through while I'm doing a reading for someone else. Recently I was doing a reading for a woman at a group show and I was talking with her mother. The woman confirmed the circumstances of her mother's crossing so we knew it was her. But then the woman didn't recognize the information I was getting. She looked completely puzzled by what I was telling her and kept saying she couldn't validate it. Then this woman behind her kind of tentatively raised her hand and asked, "Could they be talking to me?" It was *her* family member taking the mike, as it were. The second woman was given a lot of validated information—we simply cut to the chase without even finding out who was talking, just because of the way it all happened. Then the mother who was originally speaking came through and said, "Don't forget to come back to me—I wasn't finished!" This happened again, later, at the same show. I was telling the person I was reading for that the spirit speaking had something to do with Vietnam, and again this person didn't know what I meant, she had no connection to Vietnam. But the young woman next to her said she was sure the message was meant for her, that this spirit who was talking about Vietnam was the very person she'd come to the show hoping to reach.

Is there any difference between doing a reading for a man or for a woman?

From my perspective, not really. No difference. I do it the same way. I'd say it's more like each individual is different. People receive things differently. No two readings are ever the same, and no two people will receive the messages in the same way. If there is any difference, it might be that fewer men will seek out a reading. For whatever reason—maybe it's being macho in some way—more men will pride themselves on being a skeptic, and even when they come to my big shows they more often than not will simply watch and not raise their hands to have a reading. I'm always very proud of the guys who do come forward. They seem brave to me.

Gay men aren't like that—I'm very popular with gays and do a lot of private parties for gay groups. These guys aren't afraid to show their emotions and we really have a ball together. I will also say that I love gay people—not only because my beloved brother Harold was gay—and I understand their struggle. I also feel that because of their struggle, they have become better human beings, understanding differences. Empathy and sharing come easier to them.

Is it hard for you to be married to a non-believer?

It has not always been easy to understand how something so obvious to me could not be completely obvious to the person I love most. That said, John's and my relationship has really evolved. When we first met, he was attracted to a cute girl with a nice personality. Twenty-five years later, I do believe he's learned a lot in a soul sense and is more in love with me spiritually today than he ever was in love with the hot body I used to have.

John was interviewed one time and asked, "What are you gonna do when you die and get to the Other Side and find out that your wife was right about everything?" I loved John's answer. He said, "All my life, I've been a good son, a good brother, a good husband, a good father, and a good friend. I've tried to do the right thing with everyone I know and anyone I meet." (This is so true! If John got an extra dollar in change for something he bought, even if he was already on his way home in the car, he'd turn around and take that dollar back to the clerk!) "If I get to the Other Side and God doesn't judge me on those things, but only on that one question of whether or not I believed in Him, and won't let me in, then that's a club I don't want to belong to anyway."

Can the Other Side tell you if your partner is cheating on you?

Of course they can and they do. But most people will have that "knowing" and they'll dismiss it, they'll talk themselves out of it. They always know what is up and They're always trying to wake us up to what's going on in our lives. In my own life there was a time when John and I hadn't been married long and things weren't going very well. John had this regular Thursday night get-together with a group of friends—they would go to a bar, have a few drinks, talk, whatever. One Thursday he came back from this get-together and he accidentally left his wallet in the car. The next day I needed to go to the ATM. I got in the car and saw John's wallet lying on the seat. Okay, I admit it. I opened it. And there, not even tucked away, is this little scrap of paper that says "Julie" and has a phone number on it. Well, you can guess how I felt about that! But I tried to stay calm and checked in with the Other Side. I asked, "Is my husband having an affair?" And They said, "No." Right. Easy for Them to say. But things had been pretty rocky lately and I just didn't quite trust what I heard. So when John got home I said to him, "Is there something you want to tell me?" He acted like he didn't know what I was talking about. So I said, "Who's Julie?" He still looked like the light hadn't gone on for him so I told him that I found her phone number in his wallet. Now he got it, he said, "Oh she was just this nice, sad woman who came last night with Joe's girlfriend. She seemed lonely. She started a conversation with me, and to be polite I let her talk to me all night. I told her I was married, but when I left, she still wanted me to take her phone number so that we could stay in touch and be friends. I didn't want to hurt her feelings so I just took it and put it in my wallet." Can you imagine having to swallow a story like that? I checked in again with the spirits, asking, "Is that true?" And They said, "Yes." Well, even as much as I trust the Other Side to give it to me straight, I still had a very hard time accepting that this was true. Our marriage was not in good shape and I found it easier to believe that John was cheating on me than that a woman's phone number in his wallet was completely innocent. But this is what They told me and I decided I had no choice but to take it on faith.

Thirteen years go by, John and I had moved to the woods in Boonton, and I am doing a reading for a woman. Just as I touch her hand to ask permission to listen, I hear, "She's Julie. She's the one." Huh? They say, "Julie. The phone number in John's wallet. That's her." Wow. I said to the woman, "Do you remember, more than ten years ago, a man named John Bertoldi?" The name didn't ring any bells for her. I named the bar and said it had been a group of guys and that she'd talked to a particular man the whole night. Then she did remember being there. I said, "That was my husband." She said, "Really? Your husband? He was such a nice man."

I'm not one to believe in coincidences. This was a real lesson for me. This woman had come to me, across more than a dozen years and two counties, just so the Other Side could show me without a doubt that my husband was faithful to me and that I really could trust Them every time.

Just for the record, I generally will not tell someone outright if I hear she has a cheating spouse. I always say, that is not my job. I can't fix everyone. I leave that to the individual to decide for herself.

Does a spirit still have the same personality as the person he or she used to be?

Definitely! They are as constant in their personalities on that side as They were on this side. If someone was pushy here, she will be pushy on the Other Side and will want to be heard. Some men, who were very flirtatious when they were living, have said things to me about my looks or about liking some part of my body. I'm doing a reading and I'm laughing and the person will say, "Why are you laughing?" I'll tell them, "He said I wasn't a bad-looking chick," and they'll say, "Yeah, you're his type." But every now and then someone who was quiet on this side or someone who maybe never would have said "I'm sorry" will communicate strongly or will say, "I never said I loved you and I should have." So sometimes They do change on the Other Side, but it's always in that vein, like They have learned something. Sometimes a client will comment how well I've "got" someone, like I'm doing impersonations or something. But it's not me, it's Them. I'm just telling what I'm hearing.

Do people on the Other Side age?

The thing to bear in mind is that physical age has nothing to do with spiritual age. Someone on this side could live only a short time, but still be a very old soul. Conversely, someone could live to be seventy-five and still be a child in spiritual terms. On that side a baby who has died is not a baby. This spirit may come through to me as "I am the nine-month-old baby my mother lost," but this is just for the purposes of letting the person know for sure that it is their baby. People always want to know why God would take a child, but to me that's the wrong question. I always wonder about the souls who would volunteer to come here when they know that maybe they will experience a fatal illness, or genetic disorder, or be abused or murdered. But the ripple effect created by their short lives and deaths reaches so far; they contribute so much. And, of course, where they have gone back to now is so much better.

But to the broader question, it seems to me that there is no fixed age that someone may be on that side. I believe you can pick your age. I know that my father does not appear to me as an old man and my brother does not appear to me as a sick man. They are both young and beautiful on the Other Side. It's most likely that spirits get to pick the age they feel most perfect, most *themselves* at. But I do know that when a client comes for a reading the person he is trying to reach will usually appear in a form that the client knew her so she will be recognized. A grandparent, for instance, won't show himself as twenty-something because his grandchild never knew him in the flesh like that.

What might make a soul volunteer for a life that he knows will be cut short?

Usually when we incarnate it is to learn something. But I believe in these cases it is to teach something. Without a doubt, a mission like that would not be given to anyone other than a very advanced or Master spirit. I can't really speak to motivation. I have to assume that a soul who has evolved to that point has a much larger understanding than we have, and the importance would not have to be explained to it.

How can you tell if the message you convey is accurate?

The main way I know that what I've told a person is accurate is if that person is able to validate it. It really is up to the client because I don't know the soul I'm getting the message from so it might not make sense to me: I just repeat what I hear. There are times, however, when I *feel* the message and know that it is extremely accurate. In a case like that, I'll stand behind it. Even if the person I'm doing the reading for can't validate it, I'll tell her to just "put it down," make a note, and think about it later. Often when someone is having a reading it's like her brain freezes and she can't think right away, even of someone she knows very well. For most people, getting a reading is not an everyday occurrence, so maybe she's nervous.

Do you ever get a message wrong?

I'd be pretty narcissistic if I said that I never get anything wrong. I'm not hearing a voice or words; I hear *thoughts*. Sometimes a thought is clear and sometimes it's not. Sometimes I get a name, sometimes just a letter. Only God is perfect.

How do you deal with skeptics?

I understand when people are skeptical. I don't care if people don't believe me, but it pisses me off if they don't respect me as a person.

Early on, I remember this one man I'll call George who was both skeptical and disrespectful. He really annoyed me. He walked in and said, "This is crap, but my daughters made me come." He sat down and I proceeded to connect with his wife and his mother. I gave him their names, details of their lives, and so forth. He said, "Oh, anyone could get that. This is crap." Today I probably would say, Okay, thanks for coming. But I was young and I wanted to prove to this man that I was actually connecting with his wife and his mother, so I asked him what I could tell him that would impress him. He said, "Tell me what I do for a living." I asked his wife and said, "Your wife tells me that you race horses, but have always wanted to sell cars." And he snapped, "No, I sell cars, but have always wanted to race horses." I got the two switched. So I said, Okay, but don't you see that the answer was there? He refused to be impressed and still claimed that it was all crap. I remember wanting to punch him, but now I think it was one of my favorite readings. It taught me that there are always going to be skeptical people. I could have given George the combination to the safe and he still would not have believed me. Sometimes you have to learn to say "screw it" and move on.

In another case, a woman who had lost her husband was having a lot of trouble getting past her grief. Her daughter, trying to help her, made her an appointment for a reading with me. But she didn't believe in psychics. She didn't believe in the Other Side. She just thought her husband was gone from her for good. She told her daughter that she didn't want to go. Her daughter was smart; she didn't pressure her. She said, "That's all right, Ma. You don't have to decide now. You have a year and a half to decide if you want to go or not." (My private readings are booked up literally years in advance now.) Every now and then, the daughter would ask her mother if she'd changed her mind, and every time her mother said no she didn't want to go. Then a week before her scheduled appointment, she was at work, alone, having coffee in the lunchroom. The room had just a table and chairs and some newspapers and magazines that people had brought in and left for others to read. There were no windows, nothing that could create a breeze. Suddenly behind her she heard a loud smack. She turned around and saw that a pile of magazines had fallen—for no apparent reason—to the floor. She went over to pick them up and saw that the top magazine, which happened to be an issue of *New Jersey Life*, had fallen open to an article titled, "Concetta Bertoldi: The Lady in the Woods." Coincidence? I think not. That skeptic became a big-time believer in that moment! Needless to say, she did show up for her appointment and was, I believe, very comforted to know that her husband was still nearby (close enough to make a mess with the magazines!).

People's belief systems are difficult to change. I do not want to change anyone's belief system, at least not just so they will like or believe in me! I simply want to help people expand their knowledge to include the reality of life after death. There are skeptics who seem to enjoy debating this topic and they have helped me become more tolerant and understanding. Eventually, the skeptics will cross to the Other Side and then all things will be revealed to them. Then they will no longer be able to deny the truth. When I first started doing readings I was afraid of people not believing me or putting me down. But now I'm confident enough that it doesn't bother me.

If psychics are "real," why can't they warn us about global disasters?

Well, some do. The trouble is the timing. We just can't be exact about that because it's so different on the Other Side where that information is coming from. We can't make an *exact* prediction of when, and even *what* is going to happen can be open for debate.

How do you handle it if you see or hear negative things from the Other Side?

I don't really get too many negative messages. Unless someone is critically ill or very old, this kind of message is just not typical. Sometimes people who are sick or dying come to me and I'll know it. I'd never say it, but sometimes they'll ask me, "How long do I have?" And I will tell them the truth. I might say, "They're telling me it's not that long. You should go do what you want to do." On occasion someone will say they've been told by a doctor that they have three months and I might hear differently, and I'll say, "Uh-uh. You've got longer than that. At least that's what They are telling me." I try to put it in a way that will be as easy as possible for the person to hear, but I always tell the truth of what I'm hearing. I owe that to my clients.

Do you ever see that someone is going to be hit by a bus?

People do ask me that kind of thing. Like "I'm gonna fly, I haven't flown in a few years, is the plane gonna crash?" Or they'll say, "Is there anything I should know? Is anything bad going to happen to me? What do they know?" That's not the kind of thing They'll tell me because there are things we are not supposed to know. Some things They can divulge, some They can't. It's very individual, I believe it has to do with our soul purpose, and also our free will. If you're given the answer to your test, you learn nothing. Sometimes I can "sense" safety and then I will say, "They're telling me that you will be safe, so go, enjoy!"

Very early on I realized you have to be careful how you tell people things. Once I had a woman who came for a reading and she asked, "Are my children safe?" I saw fire. I said, "I don't see a house, but I do see a little flame and They're telling me to watch your daughter." She became very upset, like how *dare* I tell her this? How could she protect her daughter if she didn't know what exactly was going to happen or when? I mean, she asked me— how was I supposed to know she didn't really want to know? I guess along with talking to dead people I'm also supposed to be a mind reader. But the following summer she wrote me a letter to say that her family was having a barbecue, her husband was manning the grill and talking not watching, and their little girl was next to him and the grill burst into flames—big flames shooting up. She yelled, "Tony!" and he turned and knocked the little girl out of the way. She said she was so sorry for the way she had treated me. This made me feel better, but still, I'd learned my lesson. At all times, I bear in mind that I'm not God. It's too much pressure.

I think warnings are the easiest kind of message to screw up. I do hear warnings for myself and I know that I've been kept out of some bad spots by paying attention to them. But John has had a harder time listening to help from over there. One day when he was going to work I had a vision of him having brake trouble and I asked him not to drive his truck. He argued with me, saying he didn't want to hear stuff like that. He actually had new brakes on his truck, but didn't mention that this was part of why he didn't believe what I was telling him. If he had, I might have rethought what the vision meant. That evening he came home from work white as a sheet. He said, "Why didn't you tell me not to drive my *brother's* truck?" Turns out that even though he'd argued with me, he'd still thought about what I'd said and taken it seriously. He'd decided to leave his truck in the yard and instead drove his brother's truck to work. Sure enough, the brakes went out. Thank God he wasn't hurt.

How should we use any messages we receive from a psychic? If we hear a message intended for someone else, how can we tell that person it's for him without everyone thinking we're crazy, or without upsetting the person it's for?

I think you have to judge each situation case by case. I would never recommend telling a nervous person something you know will upset them. What's the point of that? If you feel you can communicate a message to someone in a way that they'll be able to accept and appreciate, then by all means, tell them. But the spirits aren't in the game for shock value. Even though they want to be close to us, they understand when the very fact of them, as spirits, is something that someone here isn't capable of getting his head around. Their messages are intended to comfort and reassure us. The only time they might give us news that could be looked at as slightly negative is if they want to warn us about a situation, or sometimes if someone is in a relationship that is spiraling out of control, they might acknowledge that, but it's only to offer support in a difficult time that they know that person already knows about.

Does a medium know when someone is lying? Do the dead whisper in your ear and help you read minds?

I don't want to freak anyone out, but yes, to some degree I can read minds. But if you think about it, you probably can, too, to some extent. Yes, sometimes the dead do whisper in my ear, but we *all* have a built-in bullshit detector. It's just more sensitive with some people. I mean seriously, can't you tell when someone is saying, "You're looking very well!" and you haven't slept all night, you've been sick for a week, you're maybe wearing jeans and a pajama top, and you really look like you've been dragged by your hair, through a hedge, backward, that they might be feeding you a line? For me, I prefer honesty: "Concetta, you're having a bad hair day, girl!"

Or haven't you ever gotten a bad feeling about someone, that you just didn't trust them, no matter how much they smiled in your face? Maybe for no apparent reason they just make the hair go up on the back of your neck. Or maybe you're sitting around with your boyfriend or girlfriend and one of you says something and the other says, "I was just thinking that!" These are all very common examples of "mind reading," and we all do it. That said, I know that I do have this developed way beyond the average person. It comes with the package—I have an amazing depth of sensitivity about what someone is feeling about me, among other things. I can be deadly accurate!

For example, I can think of one time when John and I had just moved into our home in Boonton. I was doing some readings at the time, but I wasn't public yet so I didn't have an office and I wasn't having people come to the house on a regular basis. We were just in the process of fixing the place up, making some changes to things we didn't really like about the house when we bought it. There was a fireplace insert that we weren't crazy about; we put an ad in the paper to sell it and shortly thereafter a guy dropped by the house to look at it and he said he would take it, but had to come back the next day with a truck.

This guy creeped me out. There was just something about him that was making all my alarms go off. He told me that he'd call the next morning around 9 a.m. and that he'd probably show up with the truck around 10:30. I knew John had to go to work in the morning, but I told him that this guy made me really uneasy and so John said not to worry, he'd come home from work around 10:30 and take care of the hand-off of this fireplace insert.

That night, John and I had something we had to go to and we didn't get home until late. I was still in bed a little after eight the next morning when I heard a very loud *crack*, like something being slammed down on my bed table. Then I heard my brother Harold's voice saying, *"Get up. Get up."* I jumped out of bed and looked out the window and I see this guy, showing up more than two hours early; I'm home alone, still in my pajamas. I thought, "Oh my God. Now what am I going to do?" But just then, John pulls up in his truck and intercepts the guy and deals with the hand-off, and sends him on his way. In this case, all of us were working together: my sixth sense; John's intuition to come home earlier than we'd agreed to; and Harold on the Other Side, waking me up. I suppose you could say that the evidence against this guy was all circumstantial, but I don't tend to wait for proof when I get a feeling like that.

Can a medium use her ability for purposes that are not on the up and up? Would the Other Side, for example, cooperate if you wanted to spy on someone?

I can speak only for myself here because I don't know what relationship other mediums have with spirits on the Other Side. My own personal feeling and experience is that as long as I'm using my ability for good They will help me. If I'd try to use it for selfish or greedy reasons, I do think They'd leave me. I think that the Other Side is aware that here on the material side of things it's necessary to make a living and I don't feel They begrudge me that. But I also try to find a balance. I try to give back. It's not about a quid pro quo, like, "I'll give back if you help me out." It's what I feel is the right thing to do. I enjoy a very blessed life and I don't like to take advantage. Could another medium use her or his ability to take advantage or do something that is not for good? I don't know. I can only speak for myself.

What kind of messages are most common, especially if someone does not come to you with particular questions in mind?

Nearly every reading, the spirit or spirits I connect with will be sending messages of love. Whether or not they were able to express it on this side, that is what they feel for us. Frequently they will wish someone a happy birthday, they'll show me that there has just been a birthday or there is one just coming up. They might express how proud they are of someone—a son, daughter, or grandchild—who has done very well at something, whether it's school, a job, or just being a wonderful person. They are proud of us when we take care of one another and are kind to others, try to help out in some way. They watch the progress we are making, the lives we are altering.

Sometimes there also are warnings. I've had many souls tell me to tell a family member, "Don't smoke!" or they might feel that the family is being too hard on a child because they don't really understand the child and they are worried about it. They'll say, "Let the kid alone," or "It's not what you think." Things like that.

In some cases, people on this side cannot seem to get over the loss of a loved one. They're just refusing to heal. It's really a choice they are making, but maybe they aren't aware of that. They're refusing to choose life. What many of these people think is that if they choose to go on living and be happy they are insulting the dead. This is not at all what our deceased loved ones want for us! We can love and remember them and still go on living and experiencing joy on this side. That's what They want for us—They get no benefit out of our being miserable and They will definitely communicate that.

Mostly They just want their loved ones here to know how much they still are loved by those who have crossed over.

Are predictions made in every reading?

To be honest, I'd have to say, not always. But it really depends on what questions the client brings to me. Sometimes—very often—the client just wants to make a connection. But others might want to know, am I going to get married? Will I have a baby? Those kinds of predictions are very common and often are offered by the spirit even if they aren't asked. They'll also say things like that my client is in good health and will live a long life—a more general prediction, but certainly valuable to know. Or they'll know that my client is going on a trip somewhere and they'll tell them that they will be safe while traveling. It can get rid of a lot of worry. Or they might say, "You're going to have twins" and I guess that could *cause* some worries!

Do the predictions you make always come true?

Let me put it this way: I believe that circumstances always exist for the predictions to come true, but we also have free will. If a spirit tells us that we will be getting married, you can bet that there is someone waiting in the wings for us. But we humans are very capable of messing things up for ourselves—even things we want very badly. And also we can make the mistake of thinking something that has been predicted is going to look a certain way. Maybe a young woman is going out with a guy for a long time and she asks me to ask her dead grandmother if she's going to get married. I tell her, "Granny says yes." But then she and her boyfriend (or fiancé) break up. So she thinks, "I guess Concetta Bertoldi is just full of it!" But then she meets another guy and he sweeps her off her feet and next thing you know, they're at the altar. Granny is validated, I'm validated. Score! Score! Score!

How long does it take from the time something is predicted to the time it happens?

There is simply no one answer to this. Sometimes a prediction happens right away and sometimes it takes years. The pieces are all there but we need to be ready. We need to be careful not to self-sabotage. We need to have an open mind and not try too hard to do our own engineering, which can often be off track. No pun intended.

Bear in mind that time has no meaning on the Other Side. On this side, we're only constrained by the length of our earthly life or the capabilities of the human body. If the prediction is that you are going to have a child, if you're a woman, this will normally have to happen before you're too old, but what that means is changing, given our medical advancements in fertility. If the prediction is that we will fall in love and get married, *that* could happen when we're singing around a piano in an old folks' home. Though usually, it does happen sooner than that!

Do you remember the readings you give?

No, I never do. First of all, I'm in a subconscious state so after the fact, it's more like a dream that you had that didn't really make any sense to you so you can't remember it. Or maybe an even better way to describe it would be like when you overhear part of a conversation. In the moment you're hearing it, you might be amused by it, or a little curious about it, but you soon forget it completely because you don't know the people and it doesn't belong to you. We really retain only the things that belong to us in some way. What does happen frequently is that someone I've given a reading to will remind me of what I said. I've gotten a lot of good stories that way! Sometimes they'll tell me things right at the appointment, after the reading, when I'm in normal consciousness again, or often I'll get letters from people I've done a reading for. So that way, the message more "belongs to me" in that the person has basically handed it to me, rather than it just being something I heard in passing.

Do you ever go to funerals?

Well I have, but it's really hard on me. They're really hard on me. I don't like seeing dead bodies. I know this may offend some people, but to me a body in a box is just rotting meat. That's not the person, the soul that was the person is gone. Also, funerals are very loud for me. A lot of relatives hover around the ceremony because basically their whole family is there—for them it's just like going to a backyard barbecue or any other family gathering. But for me, all those spirits are just overwhelming.

Do the dead attend their own funerals?

Sure they do. But it's not to check on who shows up and who doesn't or to be sure that nice things are said about them. They just want to be around family. One of the first things we are told when we cross is *we'll never be taken from those we love*. Never. We will always have the ability to be with our loved ones, literally, in spirit. Any family gathering, they are there. It's irrelevant that it's a funeral. They are there only because they love to be with us.

Are the dead upset if we don't cry at their funerals?

No, they are not. See the previous question. The dead are not sitting up on a cloud looking down and judging us—"Well. I guess I see *now* how she *really* felt about me." Or "Boy, he sure got over me fast!" They want us to be happy. I can't say for sure that if someone's widower showed up at her funeral with his secret girlfriend on his arm it would actually be *appreciated*, I don't know if that guy could actually say, "This is what my wife would have *wanted*," but even something like that, the dead would understand—they'd know all the whys about their own marriage and what that new relationship was for, too, karmically speaking. But no, tears are not a requisite. In fact, the opposite. They much prefer smiles and laughter.

Is there something the dead wish we'd do at a wake, funeral, or memorial service?

Yes, in fact, there is. They wish we'd get back to smiling as soon as possible. They want to be remembered with happiness. They really hate to be responsible for anyone's sadness. A cheerful send-off, I'm sure, would please them very much. Look at Tammy Faye Bakker—she got it! She was a good woman who had done the best she knew how and she knew where she was going. She didn't want anyone to be sad: she wanted a celebration. She told her husband she wanted balloons, and her husband filled the church with balloons! However, I'm human. I understand that is not always easy.

Can you ever turn off the chatter from the Other Side?

Not completely; I'm always with them. But it's a bit like riding on a bus where there are people all around you in the other seats, but maybe they're not talking all the time. I just don't have a lot of control over when a conversation may start. I've always walked through life feeling like I know a secret that nobody else knows. Now that I think of it, I wonder if that's sort of what it's like to be pregnant and have another person always with you, communicating with you.

In any case, many a night I have been woken up by a dead person, or persons—sometimes it's like a whole party going on. One time I was supposed to do a reading for a man the next day (he was a skeptic, but not an obnoxious one) and I guess his father wanted to get a jump on things. He came to me that night and introduced himself to me. But it didn't end there. He had a group of buddies he wanted me to meet and he introduced *all* of them to me. Then he said, "When you talk with my son, mention the glasses. He'll know what you mean." With all the people he wanted me to meet, I hardly slept that night. The next day when his son had his reading I said, "Your father kept me up all night last night. He wanted me to meet all his friends. Did he have a group of really good friends?" The guy was amazed. He confirmed that his dad had this lifelong pack of buddies, nearly all of them on the Other Side now. They got together regularly to play cards or whatever. I said, "Well, your father hasn't changed much and you'll be glad to know the party is still going on." Then I said, "He told me to mention the glasses to you. Do you know what he's talking about?" The guy said, "Oh my God. I found a pair of old glasses at a flea market some years ago that were exactly like the ones my father used to wear. I had them fitted with my prescription and I wore them for years. Finally they broke and I threw them in a drawer. Just days ago, I came across them in the drawer and I pulled them out and said to my wife, "I'd love to have glasses like this again, but I'm sure I'll never find these same frames twice." I don't believe this man was skeptical anymore.

I also see ghosts from time to time and I can tell you, if you want to have a heart attack there is nothing quite like waking up and seeing someone in your bedroom who doesn't belong there. Of course, every time *I* woke up, I'd wake *John* up and want him to go check on whoever it was this time in the closet or out in the hall. Which was ridiculous because John doesn't see spirits and he didn't appreciate losing sleep over something that, for him, doesn't even exist. He finally got fed up and decided to put in a very serious security system at our house. We always turn it on when we go to bed so if I wake up and see someone in my room, but the alarm has not gone off, I know it's a dead person and I just roll over and go back to sleep.

How are you able to sleep after being woken up by a dead person?

I guess I'm just used to them. They can be annoying but I'm not afraid of them, even though sometimes they might make me jump or even scream if they startle me. Or, like before we had the alarm, if I don't know for sure it's a dead person I might be scared. But speaking of sleeping, I have no idea whether they just have no sense of time or whether they have an exceptionally weird sense of humor, but they seem to delight in keeping me from sleeping. Even in hot weather I always need to have some kind of cover over me because they like to tap or touch me. One night there was a spirit that kept messing with my feet, kept pinching my toes. I got really aggravated and pulled the sheet over my feet and said, *"Would you knock it off?"* After that I didn't feel anything and I was able to sleep. But they weren't quite through with me. . . .

I'm a pretty neat person and I am completely conscientious about certain things. For example: my bedroom slippers. I always take them off and leave them beside my bed, together, pointing out so that when I get up I can just slip my feet into them and go. Well, the next morning I got up and my slippers were not where I'd left them. On occasion, maybe John will be walking in the room and inadvertently kick one of them and it might not be perfectly in its place, but in this case both slippers were simply gone. I looked everywhere, high and low. Finally, I spotted them—behind my bedside table. There was absolutely no way the slippers could have gotten there accidentally. The table is so large and heavy that I had to pull it several feet away from the wall in order to get behind it to retrieve them. And both slippers were neatly placed, side by side, perfectly parallel to the wall. As I wrestled the table to get my slippers I'm amazed I didn't hear some spirit laughing!

It doesn't bother you that dead people are always in your bedroom? How did you learn to be so unself-conscious?

I am always amazed at how often this type of question comes up. People are so obsessed about inhibitions, especially concerning the body. They don't seem to get it that the dead don't care. In the way we tend to think of things like this, the subject wouldn't even register with them. They're not peeking and commenting; they couldn't care less about whether we have a rockin' body or are covered in cellulite. Think about it, they're in paradise. Did God drop Adam and Eve into the garden wearing Guess jeans? Not that I recall. And as far as I know, they aren't judging performance and scoring us with extra points for "level of difficulty."

I don't feel like I'm overcoming something to not be bothered by their presence in my bedroom or bathroom. Maybe that's just me. I'm pretty relaxed about that kind of thing in general. I mean, I wouldn't show up at the beach naked. But I also wouldn't care if someone saw me in my bikini and thought I looked fat. It just doesn't bother me.

How do the dead watch us if they aren't physical and don't have eyes?

To be honest, I really can't explain this in any scientific way. Maybe the better way to explain it is to say that they *perceive* us, they are *aware* of us, our thoughts, our actions. It's not like they are peering at us; they are simply all-knowing energy.

If someone is read multiple times, will she hear different information? Is it best to have some lag time between our communications with the Other Side?

Oh, sure, there will be different messages, along with some of the same. Nearly every reading, They send their messages of love and that is not likely to change from one time to the next. But the dead are completely up to date over there, They see it all, so of course They won't tell you the same thing over and over. As you progress in your life, there will be more news available. I wouldn't suggest getting a reading more than once a year. That way it'll stay entertaining.

Are you ever concerned that clients might become addicted to readings and using communications from the Other Side to avoid living their lives?

This does happen and I would try to discourage it. We can get addicted to virtually anything, psychic readings included. We're here to face challenges, learn, be tested. We can't go to the medium for the answers to our test, any more than we should be relying completely on a therapist to unravel our lives, or be dependent on whatever a friend tells us to think or do. I think they're all somewhat in the same category—mediums, therapists, and friends—yet each with obvious differences. They all can be touchstones in life, there when needed, but to lean too heavily on advice from any of them just isn't healthy.

Do the dead know our future loves?

Of all the questions I'm asked, the most frequently asked are Will I get married? *When* will I get married? and *Who* will I marry? (Can't always answer that one, sorry!) Babies run a close second, but we'll get to them later. . . .

To get back to the question at hand, yes, they do. At one of the private parties I do for small groups, one of the women told me that she'd had a reading from me before and that I had told her that she'd meet a guy named J or James, and that they'd meet through someone named Al. She hadn't believed it, she didn't know any Al. Then sometime later, a friend of hers died and at the wake she met a guy named Allen she hadn't known before, who had been another friend of her friend who had died. Because of this connection, they stayed in touch and she even began to pal around with some other people she met through Allen—one of those people was James, and they *did* become an item.

In another case, my assistant, Elena, was dating a guy she was serious about, but I heard from the Other Side that this guy wasn't the one, that she'd be meeting a new guy and getting married within "twelve," which I took to mean twelve months (although it could have been twelve weeks or even days). She didn't believe me, but nevertheless, that's just how it happened.

Do they know who we will marry?

Bearing in mind that we all have free will, they definitely do have an idea about it, and often will even give the name.

In my own case, I was twenty-eight years old and didn't think I'd be marrying someone divorced with two children, but when I met John, They told me that he was "the one." I didn't think I'd have to take that on, I thought I'd have a fresh start, and even though I'd been told long ago that I'd never have children of my own, I had not yet accepted that, so I was not looking for a ready-made family. It was far from smooth sailing, especially in the first ten years. But I can honestly say that when I see the big picture, John is definitely the right match for me.

Sometimes the dead will give you more advice than you think you want, but we need to trust that They have our best interests at heart. Some years ago, I had sought out the services of a woman I'd heard was good with decorative painting and interior design. Kim and I got to be friends while she worked on my home, and when she learned what I did, she was skeptical, but curious. She decided to make an appointment, which at that time was only a five-month wait. When I did the reading, her father came through and immediately addressed the fact that she'd been in an abusive marriage for too many years and she needed to find the courage to leave. To her credit, Kim took this advice very seriously. She knew in her heart that her father was right and she was able to lean on him in spirit to give her the strength to end that marriage. It was the second part of the reading that she really didn't want to hear. After twenty-one years of a bad relationship, Kim could not believe that she would ever marry again. When her father assured her that she would be married again—this time, happily, and he even told her the name of the man she would marry—she was actually angry. I'm sure it sounded like too much of a fairy tale, like I was just telling her what I thought she'd like to hear. But sure enough, eight months later, her father's prediction came true. Kim's second husband had some similar issues in his previous marriage so there was a lot of understanding between them. I was honored that Kim and her husband asked that I do a reading for them at their wedding; to this day, they are very happily married.

Does the Other Side ever arrange a love connection?

They do try to help us attain love. They put people in front of you who They think would be wonderful for you, but you have to make a choice. You can accept or you can reject. We live in a society that places a lot of value on the look of the package so I think a lot of relationships never get off the ground for superficial reasons. We'll say, "I'm just not attracted to him [or her]," but attraction can be many things, not just looks. If we're making a snap judgment based on the shirt, shoes, or hairstyle, those other, more meaningful qualities never get a chance.

I've heard so many stories from clients along the lines of how their spouse died and then they met someone whose spouse also had died, and when they began to talk together about their dead wife or husband they discovered all kinds of weird connections, crazy things they had in common. My read of this is that the two dead spouses had their heads together on the Other Side and plotted how they could get their widow and widower together. Or it could be someone in their larger extended family group. It really does work that way. They really do want us to be happy!

Can the dead keep us from making a mistake in a relationship?

Sure, but most of the time they don't. We are here to make our own mistakes and learn from them. Some of us learn to be wise enough to check in with our guides and really listen to the "knowing" They can bring, and not go around operating from wishful thinking. They will try to give us signs, but most of the time, They understand that we are meant to go through certain experiences so that we get the benefit of the lesson. For example, I once dated this guy. He was extremely handsome, but he was a huge jerk. He didn't listen and he was spiritually shut down. They told me he wasn't for me, but there was a lesson in the relationship for me (and maybe also for him). Okay, here's what I learned: Some guys with perfect asses really are perfect asses.

We meet everyone for a reason, a love connection can be for karmic reasons, and They will not keep us from these experiences.

Do my ex's deceased relatives know that I'm still hung up on him? Will they tell my ex that I mooned over him for three years once we both get to the Other Side?

Of course they know. But they won't have to tell him once he gets over there because he'll know, himself. He'll understand what the reason was for the connection the two of you had. The coming together and the breaking up, both would be for karmic reasons. The relationship has to do with both of your individual destinies playing out on a field of your free will. It will have its roots in a past life, but on this side you're not going to hear, "I have to leave you because last time around you screwed me out of my business." It'll be like, "I'm leaving you because you are so annoying, you never shut up for one minute." At our deepest core, the real reasons are there, but we don't have access to them consciously, even though they are guiding our behavior to a great degree.

Is there really any such thing as soul mates?

I definitely believe in soul mates. But most people are mistaken about their idea of what a soul mate is. We have previously been related to all the people in our lives, but in different relationships—for instance, you might have been your mother's mother before or your brother in this lifetime might have been your father in a previous life. I know in my own case that in a previous life I was married to my father. I know this absolutely. We need to understand that soul mates are not always a man and a woman (or two men or two women) who meet and marry and experience the most blissful relationship possible. That's the fantasy version. Someone who is your soul mate might be playing a completely different role this lifetime; just because you never end up together in an exclusive relationship does not mean that person is not your soul mate. This time around they might be your parent, your child, your sister or brother, your dear friend. We tend to think that when we meet our soul mate, we'll marry them and the reality is that this is not always possible in every single lifetime.

Is there a soul mate for everyone?

Yes. There is. But again, we may not meet up with our soul mate every time. Sometimes we have a lesson or a life purpose that might mean we're not to be with that completely perfect soul match this lifetime. We may have to catch up with each other when we get to the Other Side. But when it is meant for us to be with our soul mate on this side it is the most beautiful and amazing thing you can imagine.

Mushy's Oma and Opa (her maternal grandparents) were just like Frick and Frack. They had been married sixty-eight years, they finished each other's sentences, they could be in a roomful of chairs and sofas and they would always be sitting side by side without an inch between them. Oma was four years older than Opa; when they first met it was during the Russian war and he was ten or eleven, living in the streets and basically starving. She was thirteen or fourteen, living with her parents, and she would bring food to him. He credits her with saving his life. Opa was very industrious. By the time he was fifteen he was earning good money and by the time he was eighteen he felt he had enough to ask Oma to marry him. He made a ton of money, but when they decided to emigrate to America, everything they had earned and built was taken from them. Once they got to this country, however, Opa worked hard and made another small fortune. He always gave Oma credit, though, for all his success.

Mushy was always very close to her grandparents and she had never suffered the loss of anyone so dear to her. Oma and Opa were in pretty good health for their age, but when he was eighty-three and she was eighty-seven, Oma began to show signs of a few health problems. One day I heard the spirits telling me that Oma was going to die. I knew Oma was having conversations with her parents on the Other Side. When I told Mushy, she didn't believe it, but she was concerned enough to tell her mother, who brushed it off, saying, "Oh, I don't think so." But two days later, Oma died.

That week, before the funeral, I again heard from the Other Side. I had to tell Mushy to brace herself because Opa was going to die as well. The day of the funeral Mushy was very worried about Opa going back home alone. She tried to convince him to go to her home with her and her husband, Bob. He told Bob, "You go home and be with your wife. I want to go home and be with *my* wife." The next day Mushy and Bob went to check on Opa and found him dead. He was lying back on his bed with his arm positioned as if he'd been reaching for something. They felt, from the way his arm was angled, that he'd been sitting on the edge of his bed, reaching toward his open window when he'd fallen over backward. It was clear that Oma had come to take him home.

I definitely believe that there is love that is strong enough in a past life that in one way or another the two souls will find each other again in this life. Even if it comes later in life after previous relationships or marriages, we could still meet our soul mate in a second or third marriage. I do believe that soul mates have been married before, and will marry again in different lifetimes. The reason for this may be a combination of things, whether a karmic lesson or simply a gift from God to reunite the pair, I'm not sure.

Why do some of us find true love and others do not?

You know, I don't have a perfect answer for that. I wish I did because this is the million-dollar question. It doesn't make too much sense a lot of the time. At least not from this side. I know total whackadoodles, complete nut jobs, who have partners and I know wonderful, kind people who do not. I cannot tell you why. I do know that there is a reason and that reason will be revealed to us on the Other Side.

One thing I can tell you is that you cannot rely on the Other Side to make things perfect for you. Believe me, They are trying. Whenever They get the chance They will try to set something up to make us happier. But we have to do our own work on this side. I have a client who has come to see me a couple of times. He came to see me when his first wife divorced him, and the next time he came, he was divorced from his second wife. He said, "Concetta, can you tell me, am I ever going to find real love?" I looked at this guy's grim face—the same face any time I saw him—and I said, "Barney (not his real name), did you ever *smile* at your wife? You are paying me money and I want to give you your money's worth. So I'm not just going to tell you what you want to hear. You need to make the effort. Until you decide that you are going to be someone it's nice to be around, nobody is going to want to be around you! It's not magic. It's just common sense. That face would kill anyone's soul." No smile equals little chance.

Besides not making any effort to be pleasant, I also find that some people can be just unbelievably picky. You have to be happy with yourself, and then, if you want to be happy with someone else, you have to understand that there is no such thing as perfection. I have seen people who will decide not to date someone because they don't like the kind of shoes the guy wears. I'm not making this up! I mean, how important is *that* in the scheme of things? You have to be willing to change a pair of shoes if you don't like them—you can always go to Shoetown!

Is there anything else someone can do to improve their chances of finding true love?

Well, again, I'm not God. But I would say that a good start would be to love yourself and know that you have a right to happiness. Look in the mirror each morning when you're brushing your teeth and say, "I love you! You're a good person!" And smile! Every morning do this—you're doing something positive for yourself, as well as brushing your teeth. Some people think that for anything, you have to work hard or it's not worth it. Sometimes it can be simple. You look in the mirror every day, say, "I choose to be happy." And smile.

Are we still married to our spouses on the Other Side?

Not in the way you probably mean. The love of a married couple is eternal, but on the Other Side they wouldn't necessarily be husband and wife, even though the love would still be there. They would be two energies that love each other. And then when they come back to earth, they could come back as father and daughter, or brother and sister, or best friends. They don't have to be husband and wife again. It all depends on the mission God wants them to go on the second time around. God might say, "You can go back with him the next time, but you'll be siblings. And I want you to join forces to teach so-and-so the following lesson . . ."

But definitely that connection remains. A man—his name was Joe—who had lost his wife came for a reading and as he was leaving I saw this image that his wife was showing me. It was like making two linked circles with the thumb and first finger of both hands—just like links of a chain. I said, "Just a minute, Joe. Why is your wife showing me this?" and I did that with my fingers. Well, he got a big smile on his face and it was like "Oh my God." He explained to me that he and his wife used to love to watch the TV show *Friends* and there's this one episode where two lobsters get their pincers locked together and one of the actors says to the other, "Lobsters mate for life." His wife had thought that was so funny and she used to make this little signal to him, linking her fingers like that, across the room at a party or whatever—it was her way of saying without saying "I love you." Lobsters mate for life, and we mate—in various ways—through *many* lives!

Can you fall in love on the Other Side?

I don't think you can fall in love, I think you are reunited with love; it's not like falling in love, the love is continuous and it doesn't die.

One of my clients was upset because her mother had died and her father was dating. She said, "He's dating a woman, Concetta." I said, "Honey, do you realize your mother is happy about that?" It's not the same as dumping his wife and getting a new one. He's alive, this loving connection gives him a reason to get up in the morning. Her mother on the Other Side understands this. The new woman might be a karmic lesson for her father, a continuation of her father's life that we have no clue about. Maybe in this lifetime someone had three wives or five husbands. Maybe they were widowed, or maybe they were divorced. On the Other Side, all the exes are there together. So often they all show up together when I'm doing a reading for someone. They want me to tell everyone that over there it's all knowing and all forgiving and all loving. That's how great God is. And over on that side, They all know why it went down the way it did on this side. They know why things worked or why they didn't or what the reason was that they were together in the first place.

What about someone who never experienced true love or a loving relationship on this side? Will they know love when they cross?

Well, first of all, I think it is very sad if anyone spends a lifetime on this side and never experiences human love, but I know it can happen. It could be that they actually were loved, but the one who loved them felt restricted in some way that they could not express the love. It could be a personality thing, or a society thing. It could be a physical handicap of some kind. There are definitely numerous things on this side that restrict the flow of love or make us incapable of communicating our love. None of those restrictions exist, however, on the Other Side. In fact, some of my clients have been totally shocked to hear from a deceased parent, for example, who suddenly is able to tell them how much they love them, how much they wished they'd been able to say it before. They can barely recognize this spirit as the same person they knew in the flesh. The love we know on this side continues eternally over there, but more than that, on the Other Side of the veil, it is *all* love. Over there, love is like the air we breathe. On this side we are sustained by food, water, oxygen—the things our body needs to keep working. Over there, where we are only spirit, love sustains us.

If someone has lost her father, will he be there for her in spirit on her wedding day?

Absolutely, he will (and so will her beloved grandmother, or great-aunt, or little brother who has crossed to the Other Side). And I want to stress that this is in no way "metaphoric." The dead are able to know about all our important times, and They love to be with us for all the highs and lows of our life. They certainly would not miss a wedding, especially their own daughter's (or son's, for that matter). I have had readings where a client has asked me this question, and always the answer is: "I'll be there."

Do the dead rest?

I don't know about power napping, but I do believe that at least some of them need to rest when they first get to the Other Side. It's safe to say, I think, that when we die we are pretty worn out—not just physically, but mentally, emotionally, often spiritually. My brother died of AIDS; he weighed only eighty pounds when he died and he was a tall guy. He looked awful. After he left this side, I didn't hear from him for months. When he finally came to speak with me I asked him where he had been and he told me, "I was in transition." I don't know what exactly transition is, but I'm assuming it is some kind of resting, like in a divine spa, that some souls go through to regain their strength. I've heard of this from others, too, and it does seem like "transition" is kind of a convalescent halfway house of the spirit world. A place for souls who need special attention. They're greeted by Masters and given help to adjust to this new existence, without being in a body with the body's limitations and imperfections.

You said earlier that souls who have had some physical problem when they crossed often want to report that they are now whole. Can you say a bit about that?

It's true. On the Other Side we all are perfect in that we are all part of God and in energy form. We are not held back in any way. I might hear from a spirit that the leg that was amputated because of an accident or illness has "grown back." But this is not literal. They tell us that only because they know that this is how we on this side picture them. They don't want to be remembered like that, with their physical flaws. I am entirely certain that after years of being held in bondage in his body, when Christopher Reeve was released and able to "stand upright" and was lighter than air, nothing would have made him happier than to phone home to tell his loved ones about it. If he'd been offered the chance to do an infomercial for the miraculous glory of God, he'd have done it in a heartbeat.

Do souls have any health issues on the Other Side?

None. At least none pertaining to the body. There it's about our spiritual health and well-being. The nearest comparison to here is our psychological and/or emotional health, such as healing our guilt over things we wish we'd done differently. But that is usually resolved very quickly once we cross. On this side we need to take into account the laws of the physical universe. You can't eat Twinkies for twenty years and expect to have no physical consequences. On the Other Side, you might be able to get away with that.

Do the living have certain illnesses to teach us certain lessons?

I do think that is the case, but it's certainly not the same lesson for every person with the same disease. And sometimes the lesson is more for, or also for, the individuals surrounding the person who is ill. It's a network of shared experiences, challenges, and learning. A serious illness does not just strike someone randomly.

One thing I want to be very clear about is that an illness is *never* retribution for anything we did or didn't do. God is a loving God and does not mete out punishments of pain and suffering. Whatever happens to the soul, the soul has agreed to allow it in order to gain a deeper consciousness unobtainable in any other way. The soul will not know every detail in advance of what he will go through, what turns the experience may take. And I would be lying to say that there is never a time when in the midst of the experience the soul was not wishing he could change his mind and opt out. There is no illness on the Other Side, so without experiencing it here they cannot possibly understand how blessed we truly are when we are with God. The fact that a soul makes this choice for spiritual growth is very different from what some have called "blame the victim," which I've heard a lot about when someone who doesn't really understand how this all works will say, "so-and-so caused his own illness" or "it's her karma."

Why do some recover from so-called terminal illnesses?

The miracle of God never ceases to amaze me—the miracles God creates, the miracles He provides or gives. Recovering is a miracle, but going home also is a miracle. We are predisposed to prefer that our loved one stay on this side, but for the person who is sick, crossing over, being whole again, and being reunited with loved ones might seem the greater miracle.

From what I know, I'd have to say that one person recovering and one person not must be based on karmic reasons. Maybe it is known that the soul who recovers is someone who will make something larger of the life she got back. Maybe she is setting some kind of example. Honestly, I don't know, but these explanations make sense to me from what I know of the way the Other Side works.

Do souls who have crossed in other centuries admire modern technology?

I'm sure they are getting a kick out of it. They must be impressed with some of the advances in the world. But also, they are involved in it. They are sending souls all the time who will be working on one thing or another, whether it's home technology or medicine or whatever. So they may be going "Wow," but it's like when *you* make something that's so cool you can't help but appreciate it yourself. It's not like, "Oh my God, look what they've created down there!" It's like "Wow . . . look what we made!"

What do the dead say about future medical advances?

I do hear that we are on the threshold of some very major advances in a number of areas pertaining to our health. They keep telling me that cures for certain diseases are right around the corner. I never cease to be amazed by the changes I've seen in technology just in my lifetime. I remember when I was a kid walkie-talkies seemed magical. Now we have cell phones that can reach someone on the other side of the world with perfect clarity—and they'll play music, and take photos and movies, and you can plug them in to your computer and send your pictures to all your friends. It's just crazy. In medicine we've got everything from organ transplants to test tube babies to clones. Again, this is a world of positives and negatives and while we have advanced technical medicine we have also advanced technical weapons, both cures and destructions, and it's up to us to decide how we use each. Where will we place our energy? It's the double-edged sword of free will.

Because I'm not a scientist or a doctor, I do find it a little hard to relate in any kind of sensible detail to what They have told me about coming advances, but They are always so beautiful about trying to tell me. There are particular diseases They have named that They've told me will see major advances, whether treatments or cures, and They keep telling me that the next generation will not suffer with them anymore. The ones they mention most often are diabetes, lupus, and multiple sclerosis. Certainly there are also others. I know that what They tell me is true, that breakthroughs on these diseases are right around the corner. When my brother Harold was suffering with AIDS, They told me that something monumental was coming that had to do with hormones, but They also told me that it would not be in time for Harold. Of course, this made me sad. But I'm grateful that the new "cocktails" that now exist are keeping others from going through what my brother went through. I hope that knowing that treatments and cures for some of our worst diseases are coming soon will bring comfort to families currently struggling with them, or for whom it might be a worry in regard to having children.

Do the dead ever help us to heal from illness?

They absolutely do. You probably know that more and more, using energy of different kinds (sound, light, vibration, and so forth) is ever more prevalent in medicine. The dead are pure energy. So this is an area where They can be really "hands on," so to speak. Just off the top of my head I remember a reading where a man's mother came through and she knew he'd injured his shoulder. He'd been in physical therapy for it, but of course I didn't know that. When I told him that his mother said that she'd been putting energy on his shoulder to help heal it he said, "Wow. It *has* been feeling better. I'd even stopped thinking about it."

In my own life, a few years ago I had a serious operation, for which I'd received three blood transfusions. I was in very bad shape and desperately needed sleep in order to regain some strength. Every time the doctor came into my room it was to say, "You really *must* sleep." Unfortunately, my body rejects all narcotics so I *couldn't* sleep. I was getting worse and worse and really suffering. I was so bad that I was at the point of thinking about my life, taking account, deciding whether I would be satisfied with my life if I were to cross right then, and I had decided that I had done as well as I knew how with what I'd understood to be my job, and that I really was okay to go. I just lay there in the bed and closed my eyes.

Suddenly I was on a roller coaster, sitting in the second seat from the front. In the front seat were two men. One of them turned around to face me, and I saw it was my father. "We needed to take you out of there," he said. "We needed to get you out of your body so you could sleep." The roller coaster car seemed to be traveling straight up. We were very high up and I have a fear of heights. My father said, "Don't worry, I'm driving. If you're afraid, close your eyes." I don't know how long we went up, but I remember my father saying to me, "Please make the choice to stay," and then he said, "I'm going to bring you back down."

The next thing I knew, I was back in my body, but I felt completely different from when I'd left. The pain was nearly gone, I felt strong and restored. From that moment I began to make a full recovery. I can still remember being wheeled out of the hospital to leave. As I was pushed toward the door, the sunlight was streaming in so brilliantly I felt like I was being reborn.

When you are doing a reading,
is there some signal the dead give you
that signifies a baby is going to be born?

Yes, there is. Different mediums will have different kinds of "shorthand" with the spirits they are in communication with. They, over there, will modify the way They communicate so that it can be most easily understood by the medium in question. I know, for instance, that there are some who will see a white flower when it's somebody's birthday, while I, on the other hand, am more likely to hear Them say a month, which I know from experience to correspond to either a significant birthday or the anniversary of a crossing. Some mediums will see a cross or some other symbol over someone's head when there will be a baby born to that person or to someone in their family soon. What I see is an image that I understand to be Saint Philomena, who, according to what is known about her, died a virgin when she was about twelve or thirteen. She is a patron of children, among other things, and when I see her I can be very certain that a child is coming.

How do children arrive here?

Babies are sent to this side from God, but they also have a lot of friends on the Other Side. As I understand it, during a pregnancy, the soul of the baby does not stay with the mother until the very last part of the third trimester. Until then, it goes back and forth, by means of the tunnel, the same one we travel through when we die, just kind of checking things out and getting used to its new situation. But then toward the end, it actually does spend more time with its new body and that's when the mother will experience a lot more activity. Finally, at birth, it completely adheres to the body.

Right from the beginning, does the baby have a mission for why it comes here?

A baby might be a very old soul. But as babies come through the tunnel, they lose all memories of what it was like on the Other Side, who they were, and what they've come here for this time. It arrives in this little loaf-of-bread size and has to learn all over again how to use the physical form. But each of us comes here for soul growth, and the souls on the Other Side support the baby's mission here. As time goes by, they'll be putting other people and circumstances in place to help wake the baby up to what he or she is here to do.

Is it true that children are more prone to seeing visions of the dead?

When I say that they forget about the Other Side, it doesn't happen right away. All mothers will tell you that they've seen their baby "relating" to something—really someone—they can't see. Like the baby will be looking at a particular spot in front of her, or maybe across the room, and smiling and laughing, maybe waving her arms, like she is communicating with someone, but there's nobody there. That is a soul that the baby knew on the Other Side who is there watching over the baby. Especially now that there are baby monitors it's very common to see this kind of thing.

I hear stories of this all the time. Clients always tell me about their kids saying that they've heard something or seen someone. One story that comes to mind is my client who told me she was driving and her young daughter was in the backseat of the car. Her daughter seemed to be carrying on a conversation with someone. She said, "Honey, who are you talking with?" and her daughter replied, "Grandma. She says she lives here." Well, they just at that moment happened to be driving by the cemetery where her mother was buried—the child didn't know any difference between living there and being buried there; that's simply where she was able to see her grandmother.

I remember another client told me about her five-year-old who was at his grandmother's house, watching his mother making sandwiches. She said to him, "Mommy's making lunch for you and Grandma." And the boy points to what looks to her like an empty chair and he says, "Are you going to make lunch for Grandpa, too?"

One of my clients got a real scare from her little girl. Her daughter, only a few years old, was saying her prayers and she said, "Is it okay to say prayers for my *other* mommy and daddy?" My client was so panicked, she thought her daughter was telling her that she was going to die. But that wasn't it at all. Her daughter had been here only a short time so she was seeing her parents from the last time she was here.

Why is it that kids have the ability to communicate with the Other Side?

Little children have been on this side for only a short time; they haven't been "tarnished" yet by our expectations of what is acceptable or unacceptable here. In a sense, they are still more connected to spirit than someone older who has been in the flesh a long time. They're still able to communicate with the Other Side, telepathically, and it's not at all unusual for a child to see a grandparent, for instance, whom they knew on the Other Side before coming here, or one who has died soon after the child's birth here. They still see spirits quite easily.

But older people don't spend time talking about the dead relatives and pretty soon children lose that ability because, in essence, they turn their backs to it. This is learned behavior in order to be accepted on this side.

Is it possible to hold on to the ability to see the dead, or do all children (except those like yourself who are truly psychic) lose this ability eventually?

I think generally this ability does fade. But like I just said, when a young child begins to turn his back on the spirits around him, it's nearly always to fit in with what he sees as normal on this side. A parent who doesn't remember his or her own experiences with spirit may humor the child, saying, "Oh, are you talking with your imaginary friend?" So the child gets the message eventually that this is not real. Or a parent may be freaked out if her child is talking about seeing someone who has died. So the child keeps his mouth shut because he doesn't want to make Mommy uncomfortable. To keep this ability alive, when a child talks about seeing or hearing "Grandma" or "Grandpa," it's important to show her an approving face rather than a disapproving face. Kids take direction from their parents. If a parent looks scared, then the child will think that it's a bad or scary thing to see Grandpa. It's like when a kid gets near the top of the stairs, she looks back at her mother to see her reaction: Is this an okay thing? Or a not okay thing? Her face says it all. I think just keeping an open dialogue about the subject when a child brings it up can keep this ability alive to some extent. With a young child who has not even begun talking yet, you can try showing him a photograph of a loved one who has crossed and check his reaction to it. There's a good chance that he will recognize the person from over there.

When someone tells his parents, "I didn't ask to be born," according to the Other Side, is this true or not?

I believe from what I've been told that we all choose our parents, but that we do get some direction from the Other Side; it's a collective decision based on how the soul can best help over here and grow spiritually. We are born to the right people and in the right circumstances to let this life's purpose unfold through our free will and our different choices and actions. In every situation, we choose. We come here knowing to whom we'll be born, that there will be a lesson (or probably more than one!) that we will be confronted by, and/or make a contribution to. We will also be expected to help others who are also coming here. It is our choice to reincarnate: where, when, and to whom. It's all a combination of decisions made with the spirit Masters on the Other Side.

Is it predetermined whether we will have children or not during this lifetime?

I believe that it is predetermined, yes. Both from my own personal experience, and from that of others I'm aware of. I believe we decide before coming here whether we will have children at all, and if so, how many. And while I would normally say that we can alter this with our free will, in the case of children, I will go out on a limb and say that this is one thing that is so much an integral part of the divine plan that there is no way we can change it once we are here. Having or not having children is a huge part of the framework of any life. I can't really think of anything bigger, even including a life-threatening illness or accident. Since each child will bring different lessons to the parent(s), I think the question of "how many" is resolved before we come back here.

When the dead predict a birth could it actually be an adoption?

Yes, absolutely. In a prediction, a "birth" is literally "a child in your arms," so it could be an adopted child or a biological birth. The result is the same. That child belongs to that mother or father.

Can you bring messages from anyone who has passed on, even famous people?

Let's put it this way: I can bring messages only from those who had a connection with the person who is receiving the reading. So if you think that Elvis or James Dean is going to speak to you from the Other Side, you are going to be disappointed unless you had a relationship with one of them. There have been some occasions where I've been connected, spiritually speaking, to someone who was famous when they were living. But in every case it has been because the person I was doing the reading for had a connection to that individual. Hey, if I could talk to whoever I wanted I'd tell Jim Morrison, "Sorry for what they all did to your grave site!"

What is different about reading for a celebrity?

Not much. They want to know the same stuff that everyone else does. They want to talk to their relatives or ask if they are going to get married, have kids, and so on. One aspect that is different is that oftentimes actors will come to me because they are looking for something spiritual to connect with that will help them with their craft. Acting is so delicate and I think it helps actors to be in touch with the spiritual world. But other than that, it's not different. Except when they offer to send a private jet. That's a bit surreal and I don't think I'll ever get used to that.

Have you read for many celebrities?

There are a handful. I've done readings for Alec and Billy Baldwin; Ed Begley Jr.; *Sopranos* cast members Edie Falco, Federico Castelluccio, and Vincent Curatola; and also Julia Louis-Dreyfus, Illeana Douglas, and Jeff Goldblum—what a sweetie! He is every bit as nice as he seems onscreen. When I met him, he gave me a hug and I just wanted to melt! I've become very good friends with Talina Fernández, whose show is based in Mexico but goes out to Spanish-language television around the world. And there's also Cristina, who is like our Spanish-language Oprah here in Miami.

I'm terrible about even knowing who is famous sometimes. There have been a few athletes and I never really knew who they were until they were leaving our house and my husband said, "Do you know who that *was?*"

Once my friend Jon Cornick, who is a movie producer, introduced me to a woman who is a music promoter. She had a client in town and told me that he really wanted to meet me. By "in town" she wasn't talking about Boonton, New Jersey, she meant New York City, about forty-five minutes and the Hudson River away. She said her client was doing a couple of shows and he wanted to send a limousine to pick me up and bring me to his hotel for me to do a reading. I knew this man was a musician, but I didn't recognize him. I did the reading and then we all had a very nice dinner together. The guy was Phil Lesh from the Grateful Dead—a very nice man, he invited me to one of their concerts but unfortunately my work schedule didn't allow me to go. You might be asking did Jerry Garcia come through? The answer is, yes he did! But the point is, this is not the kind of thing people are interested in when they come to see me—or have me brought to them—whichever. We're all human. We all have similar concerns. We want to know about our families. We're grateful to hear from the dead who are close to us even when they aren't anyone famous.

In the case of Talina Fernández, I met her because I first read for her daughter Mariana. But to back up a little bit, I owe the opportunity to meet both Talina and Mariana to my friendship with James Van Praagh. Once James became aware of me and my abilities, he was incredibly generous. He put my information up on his Web site and then I received this amazing invitation to do some shows with him in Mexico City. In Mexico, we were interviewed by magazines, radio, television, and then we did these large group shows. At one of these I did a reading for Talina's daughter Mariana. She'd recently lost a friend and I was able to have her validate that her friend had died in a plane crash. It was Mariana's deceased friend's son's birthday and I was able to convey that her friend was saying "Happy Birthday" to her son. Apparently, Mariana spoke very glowingly of her reading to her mother. The next part of the story is very sad. Unfortunately, while traveling, Mariana, her husband, and their kids were stopped by banditos. Mariana had a weak heart and the experience was so terrifying that she literally died of fright. She was only thirty-eight years old. Mariana had talked about me so much to her mother, Talina, that when Mariana died, Talina thought to call me and I was able to bring mother and daughter together. It was a very sad circumstance, but I was awfully glad I could help in that small way. Since then, I've been invited back to Mexico a number of times to appear on Talina's show. I also was then invited to be on Cristina's show when she did a special program on Talina. I loved hanging out on Cristina's couch with these amazing women—they are both gorgeous, warm, and funny! When I did a reading for Cristina, her mom and dad came through and told me about a particular photograph of them that Cristina had—she went and got it from her desk, a photo of her parents dancing. She told me she always has it with her, even when she's traveling. And her dad talked about a chain with small medals that she had of his, which she confirmed.

I've really loved having the opportunity to work in Mexico, but I need to improve my Spanish. Right now just about all I can say is *"sí," "no," "A dónde es el baño?"* and *"Te amo, todo el mundo!"* ("yes," "no," "Where is the bathroom?" and "I love you, everyone!").

What was your favorite celebrity reading?

I loved reading for Sarah Ferguson, the duchess of York, because then I got to talk with Diana. She was so bubbly and vibrant and she didn't stop talking. Diana told me to tell Sarah that she was sorry they argued about "the borrowed shoes," but she was laughing when she said it, so I knew it was something of an inside joke, not serious. And when I did relay that message, Sarah laughed, too. She got it, but she wasn't telling. I also loved reading for the cast of *The Sopranos* because they were my first celebrities and I loved the show.

If Tony Soprano were a real person, would you do a reading for him, or would you reject him because he was evil?

I actually have been in this position. When the person made the appointment, I was unaware of who this person was. He certainly didn't volunteer any information like "By the way, I'm a wiseguy." When he showed up, even though I was still unaware of the exact nature of what he did, I definitely got it that he was "not innocent of crimes." I don't know how else to put it. It was nothing specific, I didn't know for sure that he had killed anyone, but I knew that he was untrustworthy in a spiritual sense. The whole energy around him was different than from anyone else I ever did a reading for. When I asked him to tell me his name, he looked at me like I was the FBI, and when I asked permission to listen, from the look on his face, he probably thought I was wearing a wire.

Although I take precautions against evil, I guess my answer is, yes, I'd do a reading for Tony if I was commissioned to do one. This may seem like splitting hairs, but it's actually two different things. I always ask for protection from God, and that God keep evil from me and my home. No spirit who is evil and no one who intends evil is getting through. If I did a reading for Tony Soprano, the spirit I'd hear, most likely, is his grandmother, if she was a nice lady. Or his mother might say through me, "Please, son, ask for forgiveness."

What was your most frustrating celebrity experience?

Before I went professional, I worked as a receptionist. I was really terrible at the job. I'm severely dyslexic and really don't know how to type properly. I was good at answering phones and greeting people, but the rest of it I did my best to avoid. I worked at a few different companies and my favorite was the famous rod and reel company Abu Garcia. I didn't know anything about fishing and I didn't care. And I certainly never imagined that I would have the opportunity to meet Marilyn Monroe there!

I've always been a huge Marilyn fan—even being dyslexic I've collected numerous books about her, simply for the pictures, and I happened to have one in my desk on the very day that Joe DiMaggio came in to buy a fishing rod. When he walked in, I immediately recognized him as Marilyn Monroe's man (he also played a little baseball, I've been told). I was very excited, but the boss said that under no circumstances were we to bother Mr. DiMaggio, and we were warned not to mention Marilyn Monroe, *at all*. All I could do was shake his hand and say, "How very nice to meet you."

However, the moment I shook Mr. DiMaggio's hand, I immediately heard Marilyn's completely distinctive breathy voice. She kept saying, "Tell him that a stone is missing. Tell him that a stone is missing. He'll know what you're talking about." But I had been warned not to say her name, I was afraid I'd lose my job, so I bit my tongue and instead asked, "Would you like a cup of coffee?"

About eight years later, most of Marilyn's belongings were put up for auction at Sotheby's. There was a diamond eternity band that Joe DiMaggio had given her. One stone was missing. Of course I now wish that I had told him, but I was young and stupid. Okay, very young and very stupid. Not at all a good excuse, I see now. You just *don't* ignore Marilyn Monroe to keep a receptionist job at a rod and reel company!

What was your oddest celebrity experience?

Well, one time I was doing one of my big group shows in Verona, New Jersey, and I came out of the green room and was greeting the audience and was beginning to explain how everything worked. I said: "I just want to give an example, they're talking to me all the time. When you all got here, you saw me walking around the room out here. I couldn't stay in there [meaning the green room, where I normally wait before the beginning of a show]. There were so many souls in there talking with me—the room was cold! There were a lot of souls in there who wanted me to give messages to people out here. I'll just show you what I mean—right now, someone is telling me, 'Say *Lou Costello*.' Does that make sense to anyone here? I don't know what it means, but it's a guy who's saying, 'Say the name Lou Costello.'" A woman behind me raised her hand and one of my assistants handed her a microphone. She said she thought the message was for her. I asked her why she thought so, and she revealed that her mother and Lou's mother were best friends. She had Lou's picture on her wall, and when she was a kid, Lou Costello was supposed to come to her birthday party, but he died just before her birthday! I was knocked out. I said, "*Really?* That's wild! See? I didn't know *anything* about that." But Lou Costello could come through for this woman because there was a real connection with her.

At that same show I was doing a reading for a thirty-something man. I said, "There's someone here who says he's not a family member. He's a friend—someone who died in an airplane crash." The man said he didn't know anyone who died in an airplane crash. I said, "He's saying to say 'Teeterboro.' Do you know what that means? That's an airport here, right? It must be someone who has something to do with Teeterboro, maybe flew out of Teeterboro?" The man started to laugh, but it was a kind of hand-in-front-of-your-mouth shocked kind of laugh. He said, "Just before we came in here, we were standing outside joking about how maybe JFK Jr. would come through." I said, "You're kidding me. I'm talking to JFK Jr.??" In all honesty, I am positive the spirit who was speaking was not JFK Jr. I didn't want to say this during the show because I try not to make anyone feel bad, but I do think the spirit who was speaking was a friend of the man—he did, after all, say so. I believe I was confused in what he was trying to say. Rather than saying that he himself died in a plane crash, he was trying to make the JFK Jr. connection, but his message to his friend probably was not to make fun of the dead.

Can we be friends with celebrities once we cross over?

A celebrity is not a celebrity on the Other Side. Yes, they contributed something to this side, but that doesn't mean much when they cross over—no more than anyone else's contribution, since their reason for being in a body was for them to learn their own lessons. We are all equal on the Other Side. *Us Weekly* does not exist.

Can everyone hear dead people?

Yes, we all have this ability. I just like to say my volume is turned up higher than most. I am not fully tuned to this side, so that lets me be more in tune with the Other Side. From birth, I have not been able to hear out of my left ear. I have been told that this is one of the reasons why my volume to the Other Side is tuned so high. Most people do not hear the dead as loudly and clearly as I do, but I assure you, everybody does hear them. Do you know when something pops into your head or you think you may have heard a whisper? More often than not, that is the dead speaking to you.

How can someone who is not a medium connect with the Other Side?

The best thing I can tell you is you have to be open to it, have to stop saying things are coincidence, stop disbelieving that it's possible. It does take practice, like anything else. We're living in an "instant society," we're very impatient. We expect love to come to us in our early twenties and have all our relationship issues for our lifetime magically taken care of when we're still nearly a child. If we start a diet, we give it up after a week because the pounds aren't melting magically away. I don't know why this is. We don't expect to take up an instrument and play perfectly from the first note, or to be able to run a marathon just because we've managed to get our sneakers tied. What I can tell you is that if you open a window, fresh air will come in. You can open the window a little or a lot. If you open it wide and leave it open you'll get your house aired out and also have a clearer view. Same with connecting with the Other Side. You need to open the window and you need to leave it open.

I suggest that you begin to talk with them and then listen for any reply. You can ask for a signal of some kind. Ask for evidence. Say to the spirit you want to reach, "I want to see you!" But when they deliver the evidence, you can't say, "Oh, it's just a coincidence." Also, you need to be patient. It's small steps. With practice you'll get better.

Can the dead speak to us in our dreams?

For some reason this seems to confuse people. There are two different things: dreams and visits. Both happen when we're sleeping, but a dream is usually convoluted and often has a psychological root. Generally, a dream needs to be interpreted before we can get any message from it. A visit is very straightforward. It's usually short and sweet. We will see our loved ones, and we can "hear" them, we'll hear their actual voice, but the communication is really telepathic. We won't see their lips moving because they are communicating with their minds. Our subconscious mind will remember the visit, and the message will be clear. Unlike a dream, it won't need any interpretation.

Do our deceased loved ones try to contact us on our special days?

They definitely do. One man in his early forties, who I was doing a reading for, told me that he missed his mother a lot. He said that on his last birthday he could not stop thinking about her, wondering how she was, whether she ever thought of him on the Other Side. He did believe in the spiritual world, but he didn't feel he had any access to it and he felt frustrated and sad. He decided to go for a walk to try to make himself feel better and along his walk he saw one of those silver mylar balloons. It had lost all the gas that makes it float and it was lying flat on the ground. He saw that the picture on it was of Strawberry Short-cake. He picked it up to throw it in the next trash can he saw, and just happened to turn it over. On the other side it said, "Happy Birthday." He asked me, "Concetta, do you think that was a message from my mother?" Do I *think* it was? I *know* it was!

Do the dead feel what we would consider an emotional response to communicating with us?

It's a wonderful thing for our loved ones to be able to still be in touch with us. They love it that we remember them. They want to be acknowledged and to let us know they are still present. Even on the Other Side, They don't want to be ignored, dismissed, or forgotten.

Can the dead kick soda cans and walk through walls like in the movie *Ghost*?

What? Are you joking? Of course. As for walls, spirits are energy forms. Nothing is solid to Them. And kicking a can is no big deal for a spirit. They can use their energy to do all sorts of things—move things around, knock things over. They can start a stopped clock or make the hands go faster, make lights flicker, turn the water on. They never are trying to frighten us when They do these things. They just want to let us know that They're there. On occasion, They're trying to be funny, but mostly it's just to say, "hello."

How is it that the dead, in spirit form, can manipulate material objects on this side?

There is a limit, I believe, to what they can do. Like they can't actually write you a letter, but they can push things around energetically, using small electrical charges. I've had them turn the lights off or on, or turn water on in the bathroom—to be honest, I'm not sure how they do that. The only way I know for the spirit world to affect the material world is energetically, and it seems it would take a good bit of force, if not a firm grasp, to turn those handles, but somehow they manage. Sometimes they'll arrange for us to hear a particular song on the radio. It may be a combination of things how this is arranged. Maybe they are able to subconsciously urge that the song be included in the playlist, and then maybe they subconsciously nudge us to tune in at the right moment. Or maybe they just know when a song will be playing and the first step isn't necessary. I'm not sure. I think they will basically use any means at their disposal to make themselves known.

If we should be able to validate information in a reading, why isn't it always clear or obvious?

Sometimes the information we're given unfolds. Sometimes it takes a while for a person to understand the message. Its meaning will come to them later—sometimes much later. Sometimes it's like what I mentioned before, having a reading is such an out-of-the-ordinary experience that while they are with me their brain locks up and they just can't think, but maybe driving home it'll suddenly come to them what the message was about. Or it might take years, depending on what the message was. It's very individual. It's not up to me—I just tell the person what I hear and see. I do the best I can to give them any details clearly.

It doesn't happen often, but I've also had the experience of two or more people coming for a reading and one of them denying that something I told them was true. Then later they call me and say that the message really *was* true—they just didn't want their friend to know that thing, whatever it was. In any case, I'm just the messenger. Don't shoot me!

How meaningful are coincidences in our lives?

Oh my God! Don't you know there is no such thing as a coincidence? What we notice as a "coincidence" is really just the instances when the Other Side has worked with us so seamlessly that it's like pieces of a puzzle coming together in our lives in a perfect way. Often it's a case of providing us with something we are desperate for right in that moment.

Cristina, who has a very popular talk show for the Spanish-speaking community, had invited me to be part of a special show devoted to Talina Fernández. It was one of those "this is your life" type things, and she'd invited Talina's mother, sister, husband, and granddaughter, and *me*, so I could not help feeling like family. I was very honored to be there. John came down with me and we were staying at the Coconut Grove and would have been having a wonderful time, except that I had a *terrible* headache. We were in a restaurant and I was digging through my purse even though I knew I didn't have any aspirin in there. And then I begged a waiter—I know they aren't allowed to give customers any drugs, but I thought maybe he'd see how desperate I was and take pity and smuggle me one. But of course he couldn't risk his job to do that and I really didn't blame him. I was about ready to stand up in the restaurant and scream, *"Does anybody here have a freakin' aspirin???"* and I had just said to John, "I would *kill* for an aspirin," when two ladies sat down at the table next to us. The waiter handed them menus and one asked for a glass of water. She opened her purse and took out a bottle of aspirin. I wasn't shy about asking for one, even though their English was not so hot and my Spanish was worse! And nobody will convince me that that bottle of aspirin was a coincidence.

This same phenomenon is in operation when you are working on a project and you maybe hit a wall with part of it, you can't find the answer you need or the piece you need and then you're going somewhere on a bus and you "happen" to sit down next to someone talking on his cell phone about the very thing you needed to know. Even though I think it's very rude for people to talk away on their cell phones on the bus, still you get your answer and it wasn't any accident or coincidence, either. They're over there pulling strings, greasing wheels, and directing traffic to get you what you need.

Is there another word that you prefer to *coincidence*?

Well, rather than "coincidences," I think of them as validations because they validate the near-perfection of the Other Side. I've heard so many stories of things coming together in ways that seem really impossible with our limited way of understanding.

I did a reading for a woman and the person who came through was her sister. Her sister was showing me a ring and she was saying to tell my client, "with all my love," which is something that happens frequently—I'll be shown an object that has meaning between the client and the individual who has passed on and is communicating from the Other Side. My client acknowledged that she knew what the ring meant and I continued with the reading. I didn't stop and ask her what the ring meant—I didn't want to know. I try not to let people tell me things while I'm doing the reading because I don't want to lose the thread of what is going on with the communication, and I also don't want information that may color what I'm hearing from the Other Side. So I only asked her, "Do you know what ring she is talking about?" and my client said, yes, she did.

Afterward, though, she said to me, "Concetta, I want to tell you a story."

Boy, if I had a dime for every time someone I'm doing a reading for has said that, I'd have four million dollars by now! But here's what she told me:

When her sister died, my client had wanted to have some

keepsake of hers and what she chose was a ring that her sister had worn. The ring was not very valuable, but it was precious to her because of its significance, so she didn't want to wear it and possibly lose it. She kept it in a jewelry box. One day, she's looking in the box and notices that the ring isn't there. She gets very upset, doesn't know where the ring could have gone. She mentions to her family that the ring is missing, and her teenage daughter sadly confesses that she took the ring. Unfortunately, she wore it when she went out with friends and somewhere along the way she lost it. She had no idea where—they'd been to the movies, the mall, McDonald's. It could have been lost anywhere, and frankly, losing it in any of those places, they knew they'd never see the ring again.

A year and a half goes by. One day, my client's son comes home from seeing a movie with his friends. He says, "Mom, look what I found." He shows her a ring. It's her sister's ring! She said, "Where on earth did you find it?" He said, "I bought some popcorn, and when I got to the bottom of the bag, there it was."

What an amazing thing! Some would say, "What a coincidence."

Now, as I've said, in my worldview there is no such thing as a coincidence. You can say whatever you want about how the ring got into the popcorn. You can make up a whole logical story: The daughter loses the ring in the theater. Maybe somebody has the job of cleaning up and he finds the ring. He thinks, "Oh, it's a girl's ring. I'll just give it to so-and-so," a coworker. So maybe this girl now wears the ring and one night she's working the popcorn machine and as she scoops out popcorn, the ring falls into the bag without her noticing it. The customer who bought the popcorn finds the ring. It just happens to be the son of the woman to whom the ring belonged.

It *could* happen that way, sure. But I don't think you could even calculate the odds of the customer buying the popcorn and finding the ring being the brother of the girl who lost the ring a year and a half earlier. In my world, the only possible way this could happen is with some help from the one to whom this outcome is most important—my client's sister on the Other Side.

Are the dead responsible for what we consider miracles?

I think we call things miracles because we are unable to acknowledge that our normal everyday life is the miracle and miracles are really the norm. Our physical world and the spiritual world are completely intertwined. It's only the fact that most people will draw some nonexistent separation between the two that we start whistling the theme from *The Twilight Zone* when something like a miracle happens. Why is this so hard for us to accept?

When the dead want to validate their presence for us, do they always send a sign?

Yes, but we have to do our part, too. We have to remember to pay attention to the small things. It's not always a balloon falling from the sky with the message written on it. Another time, a woman had come to see me. She wanted to hear from her mother. She told me that she'd been hoping that her mother would send her a sign of some kind and even though she did hear from her mother in the reading there just wasn't enough to satisfy her—she just didn't feel that she could validate, and she was really disappointed. I felt bad, but I also thought there'd been a good bit of information and that her expectations were pretty high. She really wanted something to knock her out. Like, she wanted the house to fall down on top of her and to find the red shoes sticking out underneath or something. So all I could do was tell her what I believe—that she needed to be more open to the little things. When we are contacted by the dead, it's not like Hollywood. It's very simple stuff.

Later that weekend, she went to a wedding. It was an Italian wedding, the usual—very overdone with all the usual Italian stuff and *then* some. She's sitting there talking with someone about how much she misses her mother. Just then the bride takes the mike and says that she's asked the band to play a special song for the groom. The band starts to play "Danny Boy" and this woman bursts into tears. That was her very *Irish* mother's favorite song—being played at this very *Italian* wedding, just as she's talking about her mother. She called me to tell me that she finally got it. It's in the small stuff.

Does it work to set up a signal with a loved one so they can let us know for sure that we are hearing from them?

Sure it does—I've seen this many times. And it can be decided either before our loved one crosses or after; it can work both ways.

At one of my big shows, I was doing a reading for a young girl and she wanted to hear from her brother. He came through and had a number of messages for her. I can't recall what they were, but as I was finishing, I heard the word *duck*. I said, "He's saying *duck*. Do you have any idea what he's talking about?" She burst into tears! She said, "That was the word he and I decided would be our signal that it was really him talking to me."

Another time, a man whose wife had crossed came for a reading. He was in the habit of communicating with her, talking with her from time to time throughout his day, but he wasn't sure if she really heard him. So he made an appointment with me, and sure enough his wife—her name was Linda—came through and said a good number of things that he was able to validate. So when he left, he was feeling pretty good about the reading and was convinced that he wasn't wasting his time to still be talking to her even if he didn't hear any answer back. As he was leaving, suddenly I got another image and I said to him, "Why is she showing me this?" and I put the palms of my hands together, like you do when you're praying. Well, he got so excited—he opened the front of his jacket and took from the inside pocket a pencil with a pair of praying hands on top. He said he'd bought a coffee that morning and on the counter at the checkout was a cup of these pencils—one of those "impulse buy" type things set up near the cashier—and he bought one and said to his wife, "Linda, if you are really there, tell me something about this." He'd already been a satisfied customer, just from the things his wife said in the reading, but that was, for him, the icing on the cake.

What are some of the ways the dead let us know they are around us?

There are lots of small things that the dead will do to make their presence known. One of the most common is that they will move things. You could have a perfectly organized bureau top and find it in complete disarray, or maybe just some key element out of whack, like a photograph tipped over or coins arranged in a line or anything crazy like that.

One of my clients was missing her sister very much. She used to talk to her portrait in the living room. She'd just gaze at her sister's picture and have a conversation with her and beg her to show some sign that she was still around. But she never got anything out of the portrait. One day, after another session of gazing at and talking to this picture, she left her living room frustrated, only to hear a loud crash coming from the room behind her. She ran back in to discover a small resin plaque had fallen onto the hardwood floor. The plaque read, "Sisters are forever." Another of my clients was sure that her husband was nearby because she kept finding dimes all over the place that she knew "shouldn't have been where they were," and she felt that he'd been leaving them for her to find. Maybe there's a photo or painting on your wall that no matter how many times you straighten it, it will always be crooked. This is very common—moving some object into our view or tilting or upsetting something, or, sometimes, if they have a twisted sense of humor, hiding things we need, though I don't think they do that with things that are really important to us—they just like to see us go a little crazy sometimes for fun.

Are there other signals that the dead commonly use?

Nearly always it will be small things. You might catch a whiff of a particular perfume your mother always wore or your dad's aftershave. Sometimes it will be sounds—I had one client who told me that the whole family thought they were hearing her mother's footsteps in the house. Her mother used a walker so the sound was very distinctive. Sure enough, when I did her reading, her mother confirmed that she'd been practically tap-dancing to let her family know she was still around!

There are also certain animals, often turtles or frogs for some reason, that may appear in your path in some unusual way. Perhaps a bird or a butterfly.

If we connect something symbolically with a deceased loved one, when we see that symbol is it actually our loved one, or is it just a sign that they are sending to us?

I've heard a lot of confusion about this. If your mother always loved to see the first robin of spring, and you associate robins with your mother, then your mother crosses over and you begin to see robins everywhere, or maybe just one robin that tends to stick pretty close to where you are, that robin is *not* your mother. However, it is very likely that your mother is sending robins to you because she knows that when you see a robin you'll think of her.

A story comes to mind of a woman who came to me for a reading. She told me that before he died, her husband said that he'd show her a butterfly so that she would know he was still around her. So she kept looking and looking for this butterfly and was very disappointed that she never saw one. Then one evening she was out with a couple of friends for dinner. Before they ordered they were chatting about her husband, whom they all missed. Finally they opened their menus to order and there was a big butterfly—the emblem of the restaurant—printed on the menu. To her credit, the significance wasn't lost on her! So it's important also to remember that you never know how the contact will come—even if you think you know what you are looking for. Don't be disappointed if the butterfly doesn't literally land on your nose.

If we get a sign or signal from the Other Side, how can we reply?

That's an easy one. Just say, "I love you, too!" In fact, it doesn't matter one iota whether you say it out loud or whisper it or just think it. They are telepathic, they know our thoughts. Say it any way you want. You can write, you can sing it. They hear you, no matter what.

What is the truth about reincarnation?
How does it work?

What I believe, because of what I've been told and shown, is that we do return, over and over, in different bodies, for the purpose of learning different things. We come here in groups—there are people we have known before. Soul groups are quite large, not just a single family or even an extended family. We recognize feelings we have toward people when we first meet them here, whether good or bad, because of the lives we've shared with that person before.

It's so much more than just a "soul group," it's more like an energy field. When we die, we all go back to the Other Side. Those we've loved and those we've lost are all there waiting for us. Anyone who was important to you in your life will be there. They won't leave until you get there. For instance, if a child's parent dies when the child is just born or very young, that parent will not reincarnate before that child crosses over. They will wait for them, literally a lifetime. Over there time has no meaning, in any case. That child *will* know his or her parent over there before they all go back again.

To be reincarnated there is an agreement and a plan made with God and the soul's spirit Masters. The dead choose where and when they want to come back. It's always for the purpose of both learning something and helping others, teaching something as well as learning something.

Are new souls ever created, or are we just a bunch of old souls that keep on recycling?

I don't believe that any new souls are being created at this point. I think we are just a bunch of old souls that keep coming back here and then going back home. I feel that those souls we refer to as "old souls" are simply more experienced, maybe have pushed themselves more during their however-many life cycles in a body. Souls retain their personalities, so if you think about it, it makes sense. If you happen to be a slacker soul, you probably aren't going to get as much out of whatever time you put in on the planet because you just aren't exerting yourself. This is not to compare someone who maybe doesn't run around doing a lot of stuff but who is deeply philosophical and meditative to a slacker. It's not the same thing. You can be gathering experience and understanding, you can be growing, without appearing outwardly active if you are focused and studying in some way. By slacker I really mean someone who is satisfied sitting around watching TV, wanting things spoon-fed to him instead of trying to figure things out for himself and getting out and helping others and so forth. You can see how the soul who is grappling with understanding might be an "old soul" while the one who just comes back over and over without breaking a sweat would still be, in spiritual terms, a baby. It could also be that the "baby" soul, while it may have been created at the same time as an "old" soul, possibly didn't choose to come back to earth as often. There may have been longer periods when it was on the Other Side playing checkers or whatever.

When a child is conceived, is that a new soul or not?

No, I don't believe it is. A child is just a soul returning here for a new mission in life, a new job in life, a new experience in life. We've all been here before. We may come back as male or female, we may be any race or color, we may be born in one part of the world or another. But it's just another trip. I've heard many stories about people who visit a country on their vacation, they don't know why they have such an interest in seeing that place, and when they get there it's all familiar to them. There are also cases of very young children who can speak fluently in a language that is foreign to them and no one in their family speaks that language. Somehow, in both cases, there has been some previous past life memory retained when that soul has come back to this side of the veil and been born again. I don't know why this happens sometimes. It doesn't happen often, but it's not a perfect system. God is perfect, but anything to do with us humans is bound to have a few flaws in it.

What happens when a baby is aborted, miscarried, or stillborn? Where does that soul go?

Each of these scenarios is different, even though in each case it is ultimately a matter of the soul going back to the Other Side instead of being born into a body and living a life here. There still are lessons for the soul, as well as for the mother and for any number of people in the mother's life, anyone with an association to that baby who never arrives.

The first thing to remember is that the soul has made an agreement to come here and understands the circumstances of their coming, completely understands that they will not be here long, or won't even be born at all in the conventional sense. It's mapped out and chosen.

The second thing to remember is that there is always karma, a lesson and a balance involved. This is between the individual souls involved and God. At different times in history and places in the world it may have been accepted to tie the ankles of a handicapped newborn together and leave it in the wilderness thinking that this child would never have a "good" life because it was not in a perfect body, or that if an amniocentesis showed that a child was handicapped in some way the pregnancy should be terminated, or that if a baby was a girl it should be aborted or allowed to be born and then given away. All of these situations and decisions have to do with karma—choices and lessons—and while we may have an opinion, and can even vote to legislate our opinion if we live in a democracy, in spiritual terms we are not the judges. Only God can judge.

All that said, my understanding is that when a soul comes forward in anticipation of birth, it actually travels back and forth between the growing embryo and the Other Side. It does not take up residence in the mother and stay there throughout the pregnancy; rather, it adheres to the embryo at the last stage, during the last two months before birth.

Then, when it goes home, it goes back through the tunnel. From what I have been told, I believe there are three tunnels. There is a yellow one, which is for the vast majority of crossings, those of us who have lived relatively normal lives and have a normal amount of what we would think of as "sins." There is a black tunnel for the souls of those who would be considered "evil," those who have taken a human life. (There is no punishment we can mete out here that can compare to what happens on the Other Side to such an individual. However deserved their punishment, it is tragic.) And there is a blue tunnel that is reserved for those souls who cross as babies or the unborn. I do not really know why there is this specific tunnel for those who spend the shortest time here, but that is what has been shown to me.

Why do some people live to an old age and others die young?

Well, first, of course, we all are going to die. When and how is part of our destiny, and I do believe that there are reasons for things that we might not understand. I do know that this question, especially when it concerns a younger person, creates such heartache on this side. People want to know *why*, which is a question to be answered on the Other Side. I definitely have many of my own "why" questions that I'm sure I will be asking all my life, even though I know I won't get the answers until I cross home. Only God knows "why."

Will we ever get to the point where we no longer reincarnate?

Yes, I do believe we get to the point when we aren't supposed to come back anymore. I don't know how long it takes—probably longer for some than for others—and I don't know what it takes. There are highly evolved Masters that help spirits on the lower levels of growth, this I am very sure of. But I really wish I had more understanding of this because it's something that I'm intrigued by myself.

Are all of us here to learn lessons?

Absolutely.

For example, when John and I got together, immediately I knew there would be problems. I'd always been surrounded by a lot of caring and love from my family. But with John and his family I was surrounded by negative energy. I hated it, but They kept saying John was in my life to teach me something, They kept telling me to be patient. I used to have zero patience. No tolerance. I'd get angry easily if someone didn't understand me—I just had no experience with it from the way I was raised. On the other hand, John had experienced negativity all his life and so he was more like "just don't make waves." This made me furious because I felt like his family was treating me very badly and he wasn't standing up for me. We were really different in our approaches, to put it mildly. It's hard to say that this kind of experience really is good for someone, but for me, it's almost like I had to experience negativity to understand it. And I needed to learn to let others have the freedom of their own thoughts. You can't please everyone, not everyone is going to "get" you or like you. You have to allow other people to have the freedom of their own thoughts and opinions. So my relationship with John really taught me patience.

I was getting help, during all of this, and sometimes from an unusual place. I never met John's father; he was already dead when we got together. Sometimes when John and I were arguing we'd go to bed completely angry with each other and he'd be as far on his side of the bed as he could get, and I'd be as far on my side as I could get, like there was a wall down the middle of the mattress. Then I'd wake up in the middle of the night with someone pushing on my shoulder—John's father, Leo—saying, "Hey. He doesn't understand. But you know better than this." Then I'd go over to John and put my arms around him and he'd just melt, and we'd wake up in the morning with a new day and a new start.

Is there any way we can know what our own karma is, and what lessons we are here on Earth to learn?

We all are learning, over many lifetimes, by our own choices and mistakes. Karma is like a balancing out of the positive and the negative, but underlying it is purpose. Sometimes things that seem unfair to us, or not what we think we want, may be our karma balancing itself. On the other hand, it may be more related to some important reason for us being here, now, at this time and place.

In my own life, John is the one person I love very much and so far have spent nearly twenty-five years with. But I was not able to have children with him. There was a trade-off: no kids, but a great marriage to a great man, and for this I'm completely grateful. That's a kind of balance even if maybe I'd have wanted to find a different way to achieve that balance. But in terms of my purpose, the fact that I don't have children allows me to do the work I do. If I'd had kids, I would not have had the time, and I don't believe I'd have taken the chance. I wouldn't have wanted to expose them to any potential fallout from my being perceived as "weird" or worse. Going public would have been too difficult, and frankly, I don't believe I would have done so. Because I do believe that I was meant to do this work, that would have been a problem, so I can look at that and say, yes, there is meaning to the outlines of my life.

Although some things seem pretty obvious to the lay person,

let alone a therapist, I can't possibly tell anyone else what their lessons are. I'm not God so I'm only guessing. God is the only one who knows for sure. But I do think that if we are honest enough in looking at all the details that make up our lives, we can see a pattern and a purpose. And even if we don't quite "get it" on this side, when we cross over, we definitely will be given the reasons for everything we don't understand here.

Does our karma determine whether we are rich or poor?

Yes, to a great degree it does. But it's really a combination of things. We come here, born to certain parents with a certain set of circumstances, including our personalities, our looks, our level of awareness, and so forth. We're here to be challenged by being in the flesh, making decisions, living—gracefully or not—with the consequences of our decisions. Maybe we have chosen to be born into money, or maybe our challenge is to see if we can become rich on our own after being born into poverty. Maybe we have money, but make bad decisions and lose it. Maybe we earn money, or are born with it, but then for some reason can't enjoy it. Many a person is born with a silver spoon in her mouth, but could have an unattractive appearance or personality and can resent her wealth because she thinks it's the only thing about her that others care about, or she could use it to punish people she thinks don't like her.

Sometimes I see a person who looks like she has it all—good looks, a ton of money, a beautiful relationship, healthy kids. All of it, gifts from God. She is very fortunate. But I have to assume, when I see this, that such a person has karmically earned this by making good decisions and treating others well. If she makes poor choices, even someone who has been so blessed could lose it all. For her to have received such gifts, there was a reason; how she handles her good fortune will result in something else.

If the Other Side is so wonderful, why do we make the decision to come back?

So much struggle comes with the flesh, which the dead do not have to experience on the Other Side. That sounds wonderful, I know. But it is not ideal never to struggle. We learn through struggle. It is nearly impossible for Them to continue to learn and grow without this struggle. So They will choose to come back to evolve and to gain more insights. This is how we achieve a higher soul growth.

What do you mean by "soul growth"?

Soul growth is comparable to the education system we have on this side. Just as we continue to go to school to earn higher degrees, we continue to come back to the flesh so that we can "graduate" from one level to the next.

In order to evolve as a soul, is it absolutely required that we get along with everybody?

Here in the physical world, nobody's perfect. We don't have the same personalities and we don't have the same way of looking at things. That's also true on the Other Side, but what they have that we lack is the perspective that we are all here to love one another, that we are all part of God and as such there is no one more valuable than anybody else. What they know over there is that even if one person is "right" about something, that doesn't make the other person evil; they still need to be accepted. Here we always want to be right or get even or maybe shun people whose behavior we don't like. Over there, we understand that all is forgiven and it's not up to us to judge or punish.

On the Other Side, are we expected to atone for our bad behavior here?

I'm not sure if it's required, but I do know that many times when I'm doing a reading the spirit who comes through will want to apologize for something he said or did while in the flesh. There may have been a family dispute and the soul wants those who remain here to forgive him for his part in it, and if it's still going on, to put it aside. For example, I can tell you that John's father, Leo, was, while living, an alcoholic, and he did and said many, many hurtful things to John and his family. I know, because Leo has told me, that he wants to make this up to John. I think when John and I were having marital problems and Leo was reminding me that I knew better than to treat John badly, it was his way of trying to do something positive for the son he had hurt. As for me, I told you right from the beginning that I don't get along with my mother-in-law. I know it's not what God wants, and I do try. But being human, I haven't quite mastered that one yet. Will I have to peel potatoes on the Other Side? I doubt that anyone will force me, but I am aware that once I leave my body and my pride behind, I may be disappointed in myself that I wasn't able to raise my game in this area.

Does this mean we are meant to embrace those who have hurt us?

Well, Jesus does say that if someone hurts us, we are to offer them our other cheek. I'm not so sure I'm with Jesus on that one! I'm just kidding, but I do think this is misinterpreted sometimes. I think what Jesus meant is that we are to forgive, which for us humans is sometimes easier said than done. I do know that we are not obliged to let someone hurt us, especially not over and over again. None of us comes here to experience being a doormat to be walked over and stepped on. Even if we think we have karma with someone, maybe we believe we might have done something hurtful to them in a past life, the way of balancing that is not for them to hurt *us* this time around, but for us to do something good for them this time around. If someone is hurting us, we need to know that this person is creating karma for himself that will eventually need to be balanced. We need to extract ourselves from that situation. It's *their* lesson.

Say there's a husband who loves his wife. His friend tells him that he's seen her at a motel with someone else. He doesn't believe his friend. But then he finds his wife in bed with someone in their own home. Does he have to stay with her? Maybe they have kids—should he feel guilty for breaking up the family? Of course, he has to make appropriate arrangements with the children. He may even decide he can forgive her and keep the family together—these are all his choices, but it's her karmic lesson. On a lesser scale, if someone just treats you poorly, you don't need to spend a whole lot of time trying to figure out whether there is some karmic reason behind it. Most of the time, nothing even needs to be said. Just don't let them back into your positive space, don't give them any more of your energy.

If we've been in a karmic situation in this lifetime with someone, will we see that person again in our next lifetime?

Yes. Taking up my last example, the man who found his wife in bed with someone else, he'll have to interact with her again in another lifetime, but it won't be the same thing. Maybe next time they'll be coworkers and she'll have an opportunity to help him, make his life better, make him happy, if only for a day. She'll have a chance to repair the damage. He doesn't owe her anything. When something like that happens, we may try to figure out what the lesson was—but that's just because we're human and we love puzzles. We can't really know.

If a family member or loved one caused us tremendous emotional pain and suffering in this lifetime, are we irrevocably connected to them on the Other Side?

No, certainly not. On this side people may have total disregard for the damage they do. They don't understand the lifelong ramifications it can have in the life of those they hurt, or if they do, they don't care. They also, however, don't realize that on the Other Side they will have to answer for it. They will be made to feel the entire experience and the domino effect of all they did, all they caused by their actions, every bit of pain as the other person experienced it. Not pleasant, I'm sure. I can't tell you how often a spirit like this will come through in a reading, apologizing profusely to the person she hurt on this side. It's interesting that their energy is very different from the regular spirit with regular not-so-good deeds in this life. Whereas most spirits appear to me as bright clear light, someone who is guilty of crimes or cruelty will be of an energy that is darker and grayish. Maybe the person he hurt is in therapy the whole rest of her life, maybe that person can never trust anyone or can never have a normal loving relationship, she's been hurt so bad. Over there he wants to atone. He will apologize profusely to the person's very core because he knows he has done damage that deep.

Do we have to accept their apologies?

No. We don't. We're human; we're not expected to be saints. We can just live with knowing that those souls are paying for what they did to us. It is my belief that on the Other Side we will forgive, but I'm not going to try to convince someone on this side, who is still in the body and still dealing with the pain that this is the case. When we get over there, we'll each have our own experiences. Until then, we have to do our best to try to live as fully and well as we can without putting the burden of sainthood on ourselves.

Is there any kind of hierarchy in the afterlife?

I believe there are many levels on the Other Side. These levels have a definite connection to the way we led our lives here and to the advancing stages of our spiritual growth. There are different levels of accomplishment and understanding. The superior soul of God is the pinnacle.

Is there a reason why we meet every single person we meet in this life?

Everyone we meet in our lives we have met before. Everyone who comes in and out of our lives we have known before. It could have been a very brief meeting or relationship because the meeting was only to facilitate getting you from point A to point B, or the lesson in the relationship was learned quickly. Someone might be a gas station attendant you barely know in this life and be your brother in the next life. There is a deep knowing in all of us but normally we move right along without recognizing these things. Still, in the core of our being, something recognizes these truths. It's not a bad idea, every now and then, to stop and think about someone you've met and consider who that person might really be to you. I think we would treat one another a lot better if we did consider that the person next to you on the subway might have been a dear relative in another life.

What is a spirit Master?

I honestly don't know if each person has the same Masters. I don't know who the Masters are. I know that they are very "evolved" energy. To explain what I mean by "evolved," I always say it's like someone who has completed grade school, high school, college, and graduate school; they have their master's and their doctorate. You expect one thing from someone who has completed fourth grade. You expect a lot more from someone who is better educated, with advanced degrees. Different Master souls help with different difficult situations.

Are you afraid of death?

Absolutely not. I'm not afraid of death, I'm afraid only of how I will die. I am human and it's only normal. Going home and going back to the Other Side is not something to fear. I don't have any fear whatsoever about meeting my father and brother, who are there before me, and my other relatives who I have long since forgotten. I've heard of them and I know they are there. I'm not afraid of death, but I'm afraid of being alone and not having someone to love me here. John is half of my life. I have no children of my own so John and I have become such a "unit" together. Like most people, I fear being alone and unloved. On some level, I'm ashamed of this fear. I should know better. I meet so many brave people who have lost their spouses and I admire them because so often I think about what I would do in their position. Sometimes the fear is so great that it makes me wish I would die first. It's a selfish thought, but it's true.

Have you ever worked with the police to help solve a case?

Yes, I've worked with the police a few times. Once the police in a nearby town could not find a young man after searching for a few weeks. A detective in Cedar Grove, New Jersey, called and asked me if I could tell her if the young man had died. I said yes. I was told that he was dead, he was in a car, and he was in water. I also heard that they would find him in "two." Whether that meant two days, two weeks, or two months I couldn't tell. But they found him in two weeks, under a bridge. He had driven his car off the bridge and drowned.

Another time the police called about a young man who had disappeared without a trace. I told them that this young man was alive, but there were drugs involved in his disappearance. I heard that they would find him in "three." Three days later, he called home from a crack house in Los Angeles.

I do a lot of work in Mexico and there are a lot of missing persons there. I haven't worked with the police there, but I have done readings for people who have lost family members and may not know if their loved ones are alive or dead.

How do you feel about fictional television shows that portray mediums?

I'll be honest, I don't watch much television, but I always think it is fantastic when Hollywood works with those who actually have the gift to help to portray the experience in a way that feels legitimate and respectful.

In the past, television shows and movies did a lot of crap that was entertaining (people coming back from the dead covered in blood and all that stuff) but was not how the dead really come through. They're not interested in terrorizing and tormenting the living. They come through very peacefully and their intention is purely to give messages and try to help those on this side. They especially seem to get it right on *Medium* and I think Patricia Arquette really understands what it is to be born with my gift. You can tell that chick did her research.

Is it troubling to you to hear the dead all the time?

Mostly I feel extremely lucky to have been blessed with this ability. But it can be difficult, especially, as I've said, at bedtime. I hear them walking up and down stairs, laughing and talking. They are always all around me. But if I ever really need peace and quiet, I do have the ability to say, very simply, "Please, in the name of God, be gone." I will say this only when I feel the need to be quiet and by myself. At those times, this call for God's protective love is enough to still the voices. But I've become so used to this connection that I sometimes have a hard time staying on this side. At night sometimes I will astral-travel and leave my body to go visit the Other Side. When I'm there, I always want to stay, but my father and my brother always tell me I have to come back. I'm not finished with my work on this side.

Can you explain astral-travel?

Astral-travel is the act of a soul leaving its body to visit the Other Side. Our souls can leave our bodies either by slipping out through our feet or by lifting up when we are lying flat on our backs. When I plan to astral-travel, I fall asleep flat on my back so that it is easier for my soul to leave. My soul then stands in front of the window in my bedroom and I can step out into the Other Side. I *never* leave through my bedroom door because my hallway tends to be full of ghosts, usually either those who have visited with my clients that day or those who know that a loved one will be visiting me the next day and are showing up early. I just don't want to see them when I'm in that state.

From my bedroom window I have seen the most beautiful scenes: snowcapped mountains that go on forever, beautiful beaches with the whitest sand and the bluest water, endless fields of flowers as far as the eye can see. When I step out into the Other Side, I step into another dimension. There are so many planes that I never know exactly what I will see. Most often I am floating in a white room with all of my relatives who have passed on.

Do you have to be a medium to step outside of your body?

No, no. Everyone has stepped out of their bodies from time to time. Do you know the feeling when you are sleeping and you feel like you are falling out of bed? Or when you wake up and feel paralyzed and you try to scream and no sound comes out? In these cases, your soul has woken up before your body. When this happens you should visualize bringing your fingers together and think, "Please, God, bring my body back to my soul," and you will wake up completely.

What is your favorite aspect of being a medium?

Oh, there are so many parts of my job that I love. I love making sure people know there is life after death. I love getting across the message that we all belong to one another. I love telling my clients that the most important gesture in life and death is a smile.

What is one of the most important lessons you have learned as a medium?

I can tell you a few things that I've learned as a person. I've learned to consider each moment precious and to not waste one, to not waste *anything*. I've learned to pick up litter, even if I'm not the one who dropped it, to keep this world as beautiful as it can be, even if it will never be as perfect as God made it. I've learned to keep a positive attitude and any time I'm feeling angry or at all sorry for myself for *any* reason to ring the bell and say, "Snap out of it, girlfriend." Life is far too precious to waste moping.

As a medium, I've learned how important it is to step outside your own body—and I don't mean astral-travel—and see what you are doing wrong. You don't have to be a medium to do this. Anyone who is really interested in learning from his or her life can do this. Also, being a good listener is important. Listen to those you trust, whether it's your mother, your sister, or your best friend—that person will be truly honest. The dead can be brutally honest, but it's because they love us so deeply. It's good to have these kinds of friends on both sides of the veil. If you really want to learn something, brutal honesty can be a very good thing.

Do the dead ever give you winning lottery numbers?

To be honest, I'm really not interested in knowing them. That is not what I choose to use my ability for. But I *do* know when I'm going to win a raffle! I love this story:

There's a wonderful little family-owned restaurant in Boonton called Top of the Park—it's run by a nice Italian couple and their two kids and the food is great. Every Easter they raffle off a huge Perugina chocolate egg. When I say huge, I mean *huuuuge*—this egg stands around five feet high! So one April I bought five raffle tickets for ten bucks. As I bought the tickets, I heard whispering—They are telling me that I'm going to win! So I said, "Joe, I'm gonna win this egg," and he just laughed. I'm sure everyone says that. So I said, "When I win this egg, I'm going to share it with everyone." He said, "Oh, that's nice." Of course, he didn't believe I had any more chance than anyone else.

So the day comes and the priest does the drawing. He pulls out a ticket and reads out my name. Just like They told me, I won the egg. I didn't forget what I'd told Joe—I had him get a hammer and we gave that egg a whack and shared chocolate with everyone in the restaurant.

That was all fine, everyone was happy. But then Joe got curious about my saying that I was going to win. He said, "Let's just see who would have won if it wasn't you, Concetta." There were about 450 tickets in the bowl. He reached in and pulled another one out. My name was on it. Wow. That was quite a coincidence! We were all laughing. So then Joe reached in and pulled out another ticket. Oh my God. It was my name again! He reached in again, and for the fourth time—it was me! Now he was spooked—he didn't want to pull again!

If a dispute arises when the estate of someone who has crossed is being settled, do they get involved in it? Do they take sides?

They don't take sides. They have no use for or attachment to any physical thing, and certainly not money. But this does come up in readings frequently. Sometimes they will express disappointment or they'll ask me to tell my client to "let it go" if it's something that has been troubling her. On the other hand, they'll just as often refer to a specific item they used to own that they know my client has and they'll say they're glad she's kept that thing. Or they'll refer to the way their belongings were split up among the family and say how proud of their kids they are, that they went through that process without bickering or starting World War III. They don't take sides, but they do give us points for good behavior.

Has anyone ever ended a friendship with you when you revealed you could talk with dead people? If so, how did you cope?

I can think of one time when I was a child and lost a friend over my ability. I was about eleven years old and I was invited to the home of a little girl in my class named Ingrid. Ingrid was very smart and pretty; all the teachers liked her and her classmates adored her. I was no exception; I was in awe of her. Being invited to her home to play after school was a big deal to me and even more of a big deal, her parents invited me to stay to dinner. Unfortunately, I had not yet learned that I sometimes needed to screen the things I heard and knew. As I sat at their dining table, Ingrid's deceased grandmother (her father's mother) began telling me things about her family. It seemed only natural that I would turn to Ingrid's father and try to tell him what his mother was saying, but his reaction, while not dramatic, was distressing to me. I don't think Ingrid or her siblings even realized that anything had happened as her father got up from the table and beckoned for his wife to follow him into the kitchen. They called my parents to come and get me, and from that day on I was not allowed to play with Ingrid again. I was never again invited to their home and I do believe from what I heard through the grapevine that they went around the neighborhood and spoke of me as the "weird child." For a kid it was a really horrible experience. I don't think there's really any way to cope with something like this. You just have to move on; you can't change what someone believes. I was lucky to have my own parents who gave me such support, and the spirits on the Other Side always bucked me up whenever I had a problem.

Have people ever ended their relationships with you because they thought your dealings with the Other Side were unnatural?

Certainly. I had some cousins, who, forgive me for saying, weren't the nicest people. They were dishonest on many different levels and they treated people terribly—I don't even want to say some of the things they got into. But just like everybody else, they wanted readings whenever they lost someone near to them, and I obliged—they were family. Then they "found Jesus"—who, by the way, probably didn't even know He was lost—and they became "Christians." Next thing you know, I'm persona non grata with them. They don't like that I talk to the Other Side. Before, of course, they didn't mind. But now that they have religion, they decide that I'm evil. They say, We don't want to see you, we don't want to talk to you. While you're at it, take our names off your Christmas card list. One of them even let me know that *he* was the only one who could talk to the Other Side because *he* was an ordained minister! Again, the souls on the Other Side help me to cope, to move on, and to enjoy the friends and family who *do* want to be part of my life.

Would you say you are "anti-religion"?

I wouldn't like to say that I'm anti-religion. For some people religion works, it is a good support for them. For me, however, there's a difference between being religious and being spiritual.

If I can, I want to be an example to other people. I have no problem using my own life as an example. I'm no paragon of virtue. I wasn't born perfect and I'm not perfect now. But I can honestly say that I'm a spiritual person. The difference between a spiritual person and religious leaders is that many of them will have you believe that they're perfect.

God knows my heart. If it wasn't okay with God for me to do this work I wouldn't be able to do it. All I'm doing is bringing peace to people, healing them, helping them to feel better. I'm not asking for a big check like some TV minister and I'm not telling someone, "Well, if you bring me a chunk of hair I'll do a spell to remove your hex." I simply believe in God. Big time.

Does prayer save us or simply hold us captive?

To tell you the truth, I think that prayer is a beautiful thing. I think it is like meditation. To me they really are much the same. You calm yourself and say a sweet prayer with all your heart and your love. How could that be anything but good? Does it hold us captive to love? What's so terrible about that?

What is the benefit of discovering the truth about the Other Side?

Understanding that life goes on in spirit after our physical death does so many positive things for us. It heals us. It gives us peace, comfort, and knowledge to help us have better lives, learn lessons easier, live happier, and help others. It can inspire us to make changes that might be difficult because we know it really does matter. It's not just this one lifetime; the way we spend our energy has an unimaginable ripple effect in this world and the next over many lifetimes. Understanding is important on both sides of the veil. It affects the quality of our lives, the quality of our love, and the quality of our relationship, now and always, with God.

Do the dead know the secret to happiness here?

It's not that happiness has to be created in our lives. Happiness is our natural state. The difficulty is in ridding ourselves of what causes us unhappiness—most of which is of our own doing and choosing.

You have to look at your life as if it has chapters. I was always happy. But at different times there were things going on that tried to break my happiness. It's really up to us to choose happiness. You can't expect anyone else to do it for you. We have the power to bring ourselves back after a big disappointment or great loss. We are not meant to wallow in grief or punish ourselves—They don't want that. It does nothing for us.

There were some big plans that I had been told were going to happen for me, a lot of things. And I kept trying and trying to make them happen, but it wasn't the right time. I kept having all these things that came really close and then just didn't happen. The last one was so disappointing—I'd been through it all so many times and each time I'd tried to keep a good attitude, but finally I just thought, "Well, what's the matter with me? I can't seem to pull this off. Maybe I'm not supposed to have this." I was feeling very down on myself, like I wasn't good enough. I gave myself basically a couple of weeks to just mope around—which is not really like me, but I was just so frustrated and disappointed and I let it affect my self-esteem. Then I heard my father telling me that I had to stop being like that. He gave me a way to get rid of all the bad feelings. (My friend Ginger, who is a therapist, says something similar): Instead of taking a pill or having a drink or a cigarette, take a minute for yourself and visualize all the things that are bugging you. Visualize putting them in a big black garbage bag, tying it up, and dragging it to the dump. A lot of people will say, "Oh that won't work for me." But you have to try it. Just give yourself that minute—it really doesn't take long. Just visualize putting all your grief and negativity, all the stuff that's bothering you in a garbage bag and dumping it. You'll be amazed. It works.

If you had your life to live over and you could choose whatever life you wanted, would you change anything?

That's a difficult question. If I'd been given the choice when I was younger either to keep the ability I have or to have a baby, I know I would have given up this ability in a heartbeat. I've already said that I now realize that having a child would have made it impossible—in my mind, anyway—to go public with this work. But now, at the age I am, and seeing all the good I've been able to do for people by helping them connect with their loved ones who have crossed, I honestly don't know if even having a baby would have been equal to this. I feel very torn on this question—I'll have to get back to you on this one.

Any final words of wisdom?

Have confidence. You only need to believe in yourself. You have everything you need to have everything you want. Believe it. You need to keep things in perspective in this lifetime and appreciate what you have. You can't focus on what you don't have or what you feel is wrong in your life. And if I could tell you just one thing that will make the biggest improvement in the quality of your life and in the lives of everyone around you, it is this: SMILE!

ACKNOWLEDGMENTS

(in alphabetical order—you're all first with me!)

- Richard Arlook—What can I say, from the first time I met you I knew you were a Mensch. I will forever be in debt to you for all your help. Thank you from the bottom of my pancreas.
- My husband, John Bertoldi (a.k.a. Johnny Fontaine)—Thank you for believing in me when it was not easy to! Thank you for holding a light in front of me. Thank you for carrying my bags and cooking for me. Thank you for loving me always.
- My stepchildren, John and Darlene Bertoldi and Jessica and Lorenzo Franchina, and my grandchildren, Alexander, Julia, and Isabella—Thank you, my children, for understanding my crazy schedule and for all your love and support. I love you all.
- Jon Cornick (a.k.a. Corndog)—My hero, My friend. . . . I love you and thank you.
- Cornelia DiNunzio (a.k.a. Mushy)—My girlfriend, my sister for almost fifty years of sharing our lives, loves, and losses. You could never be replaced. I love you with all my heart.
- Stephany Evans—My adorable literary agent and friend (the best in the business). How can I ever thank you enough? I love you and thank you forever.
- My mother, Eleanor Ferrell—You are a great mother and have given me great advice. I have admired your intelligence all my life. Thank you for putting up with your undeniably different daughter. I love you always.
- My brother Robert and sister-in-law Choi Ferrell and my beautiful niece, Bobbie Concetta (a.k.a. the Chinese Chick)—I'm

grateful for the namesake and for your patience and support. I love you all very much.

- Ginger Grancagnolo (a.k.a. Gingerbread)—My search engine, my friend—Thank you so much for your wonderful help. I love you.

- Hope Innelli—Thank you for being so inventive in the promotion of this book. HarperCollins is fortunate to have young brilliant talent like you.

- Elena Oswald (a.k.a. My Sweet Elen Baby) who has kept me calm and protected when I have been overwhelmed and a bit nuts—Thank you honey! I love you.

- Jennifer Pooley—My adorable young editor from Harper-Collins. Thank you for remembering my story and calling me back because you believed in me. You have been wonderful and without you this book wouldn't have happened.

- Sarah Self—I would like to thank Sarah for enjoying our conversations and bringing me to the best agent ever. Without Sarah I would not have found Stephany Evans, Sarah you are a sweetheart. Thank you with all my heart.

My array of clients—Thank you for trusting me, believing in me, and allowing me to share your heartfelt stories and lives.

To my many other friends and family, I would just like to say thank you for caring about me and loving me.

My deepest thanks to Carrie Kania and David Roth-Ey at Harper Paperbacks—Thank you for saying yes, and for your incredible support for this book. My heartfelt thanks to Mauro DiPreta, Jennifer Civiletto, May Chen, Carrie Feron, and Samantha Hagerbaumer for your passion and determination to bring my book to HarperCollins, and to Nicole Reardon and Robin Bilardello for your expertise.